Grand Canyon's
NORTH RIM
and Beyond

**A Guide to the North Rim
and the Arizona Strip**

By Stewart Aitchison

GRAND CANYON
ASSOCIATION

Grand Canyon Association
Post Office Box 399
Grand Canyon, Arizona 86023-0399
(800) 858-2808
www.grandcanyon.org

Project management and editing by
        Frazier Enterprises, Inc., Sedona, Arizona
Design, maps, and production by
        Amanda Summers Design, Prescott Valley, Arizona
   Printed in Canada on recycled paper using vegetable-based inks

First Edition 2008
13 12 11 10 09   2 3 4 5

ISBN-13: 978-0-938216-92-6

Library of Congress Cataloging-in-Publication Data
Aitchison, Stewart W.
  Grand Canyon's North Rim and beyond : a guide to the North Rim and the
Arizona Strip / by Stewart Aitchison. -- 1st ed.
      p. cm.
  Includes bibliographical references and index.
  ISBN-13: 978-0-938216-92-6 (pbk.)
  1. Grand Canyon (Ariz.)--Guidebooks. 2. Grand Canyon National Park
(Ariz.)--Guidebooks. 3. Arizona Strip (Ariz.)--Guidebooks. 4. Natural
history--Arizona--Grand Canyon. 5. Natural history--Arizona--Arizona Strip.
6. Grand Canyon (Ariz.)--History. 7. Arizona Strip (Ariz.)--History. I.
Title.
  F788.A39 2008
  917.91'320454--dc22

                         2008000818

The Grand Canyon Association is a nonprofit educational organization
dedicated to cultivating knowledge, discovery, and stewardship for the
benefit of Grand Canyon National Park and its visitors. Proceeds from
the sale of this book will be used to support research and education at
Grand Canyon National Park.

TABLE OF CONTENTS

This book is dedicated to my daughter Kate and to the next generation of Grand Canyon explorers.

FRONT COVER:
Mt. Hayden as seen near Point Imperial

Grand Canyon's
NORTH RIM
and Beyond

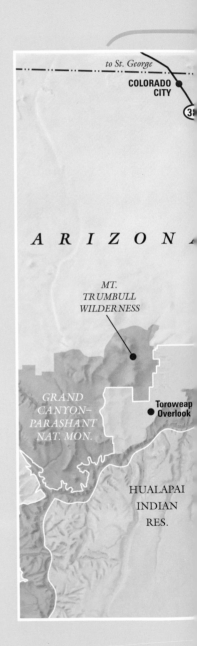

PAGE 54

PAGE 62

PAGE 78

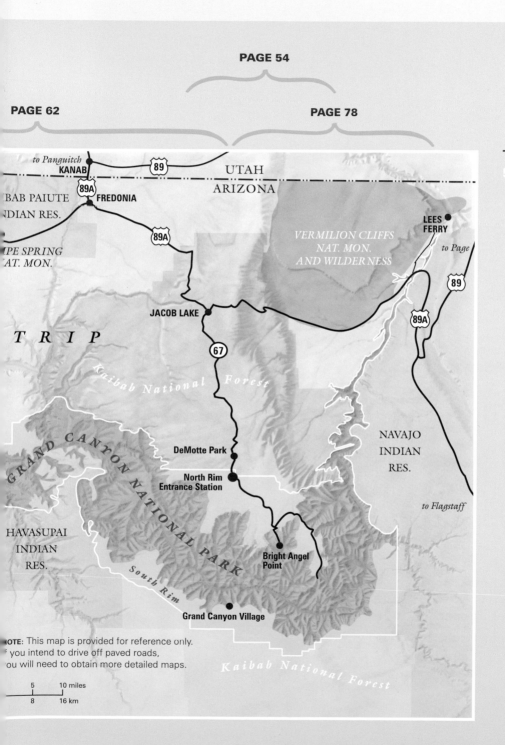

to Panguitch
KANAB
89
UTAH
ARIZONA

KAIBAB PAIUTE
INDIAN RES.
89A
FREDONIA

89A

VERMILION CLIFFS
NAT. MON.
AND WILDERNESS

LEES
FERRY

to Page

89

PE SPRING
AT. MON.

JACOB LAKE

89A

67

T R I P

Kaibab National Forest

NAVAJO
INDIAN
RES.

to Flagstaff

GRAND CANYON NATIONAL PARK

DeMotte Park

North Rim
Entrance Station

HAVASUPAI
INDIAN
RES.

South Rim

Bright Angel
Point

Grand Canyon Village

NOTE: This map is provided for reference only.
If you intend to drive off paved roads,
you will need to obtain more detailed maps.

5   10 miles
8   16 km

Kaibab National Forest

5

How to Use this Book

Although you may certainly choose to read this book from cover to cover (and I hope that you do), you're probably on vacation and just want a little information about what you are seeing as you tour the Grand Canyon's North Rim and the Arizona Strip. This book enables you to learn as much or as little as you like and in whatever order you choose because each story is complete in and of itself. You may read from front to back, back to front, or skip around to whatever interests you.

The maps included here are intended to orient you to your surroundings and your options. They are not detailed enough to guide you around once you leave paved roads. If you intend to explore the maze of dirt roads on the Arizona Strip you will need better maps! Equip yourself well, for there are no services off pavement and cell phone coverage is spotty at best.

Following the Introduction, the book is divided into two parts. The first part covers the roads and stops within Grand Canyon National Park. The second part includes the main approaches to the North Rim.

Refer to the index map on pages 4 and 5 to orient yourself; find your current location, define your route, and begin to discover the North Rim and beyond.

Summer storm along the road to Cape Royal

Introduction

I love the North Rim of the Grand Canyon.
Approaching the rim takes you through one of the most
enchanting forests in the American Southwest. Even without
the great gorge, the Kaibab Plateau is worth visiting; the
canyon is an added bonus. The North Rim is also the quiet
side of the great chasm. Whereas nearly 5 million people visit
the South Rim each year, less than one-tenth that number
make it to the "other side." Part of the reason for this is that
the North Rim is not on the way to some large population
center. Travelers along Interstate 40, driving from the West
Coast to the East and visa versa, often make the short detour

*Quaking aspens
blaze orange
and gold in the
shortening days of
autumn.*

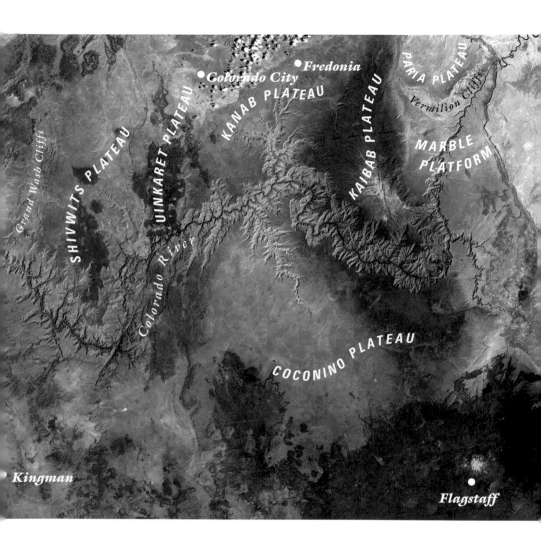

The Grand Canyon as seen from space

up to the South Rim for a quick look at the canyon. But the North Rim is off the beaten path; it takes extra planning and time to get there. Another major reason that the North Rim receives fewer visitors is that the highway leading into the park is usually closed from late November until mid-May, nearly half of the year, by deep snow.

No matter from which direction you approach the North Rim of the Grand Canyon, you must traverse part of the Arizona Strip, nearly 5 million acres (2 million hectares) of the emptiest territory in the lower forty-eight. Topographically, the Arizona Strip can be broken into seven major subdivisions: the Marble Platform, the Paria, Kaibab, Kanab, Uinkaret, and Shivwits plateaus, all subdivisions of the greater Colorado Plateau, along with a slice of Basin and Range country farther west. Going west from the Colorado River (entrenched in the deep Marble Canyon), the relatively flat desert of the Marble Platform rises like a giant cresting wave to become the high, forested Kaibab Plateau. The Marble Platform is bounded on the north by the southern escarpment of the Paria Plateau—the dramatic Vermilion Cliffs.

On the west side of the Kaibab Plateau, the land drops back into arid country in a series of dramatic steps to form the Kanab, Uinkaret, and Shivwits plateaus. The far west side of the Shivwits Plateau drops off where the Grand Wash Cliffs mark the edge of the Colorado Plateau and the beginning of the Basin and Range Province. The sedimentary rock layers of the Arizona Strip are essentially the same ones exposed in the walls of the Grand Canyon. Capping some of these rocks are thick layers of volcanic basalt and cinders.

Only a few small towns and scattered ranches exist on the vast, 11,000-square-mile (28,488-sq-km) Arizona Strip, an area the size of Massachusetts: Colorado City, famous, or perhaps notorious, as a community of polygamists; Moccasin on the Kaibab Indian Reservation; Fredonia, a quiet, friendly ranching

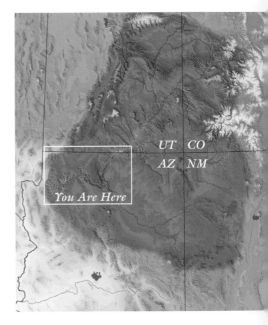

The Grand Canyon lies within the physiographic province known as the Colorado Plateau, which spans the Four-Corners region.

WEATHER FACTS

At the Bright Angel Ranger Station on the North Rim, a frigid winter low of -22°F (-30°C) has been recorded. Fewer than 8 miles (13 km) away at Phantom Ranch, near the Colorado River, summer temperatures can soar to a scorching 120°F (49°C) or more. And that's in the shade! The North Rim averages 26 inches (66 cm) of precipitation annually, about half of that coming in the form of snow. Snowfall averages 142 inches (360 cm) per year, with a record of 272 inches (691 cm) falling in 1978. The South Rim, a good thousand feet (305 m) lower than the north side, averages only 58 inches (147 cm) of snow and Phantom Ranch receives less than 1 inch (2.5 cm). Lees Ferry is the driest part of the Arizona Strip, averaging a withering 6.1 inches (15.5 cm) of rain per year.

outpost and, with about 1,300 residents, the largest town on the strip; and Littlefield, a farming community along Interstate 15. Marble Canyon, Vermilion Cliffs, Cliff Dwellers, Jacob Lake, Kaibab Lodge, and Grand Canyon Lodge are all too small to qualify as villages but do offer lodging, meals, and a few basic services, at least seasonally.

What is typically thought of as the North Rim is the southern extension of the Kaibab Plateau. The name Kaibab is generally translated as "mountain lying down," an apt description of the high plateau that is relatively flat on top. Kaibab is likely derived from the corruption of the Southern Paiute word *Kaivavitsets*, which refers to the Mountain Lying Down People (or Kaibab Paiute People).

Early settlers usually called the plateau Buckskin Mountain, referring to numerous mule deer living there. However, Frederick Dellenbaugh, one of explorer John Wesley Powell's men, thought that the Buckskin name was derived from the plateau's resemblance to a skin stretched out on the ground. Whatever the exact origin of these names, the Kaibab Plateau is indeed a "mountain lying down" covered with beautiful forests alive with deer and other wildlife.

The Grand Canyon is an effective barrier between most of Arizona and the northwest corner of the state—the Arizona Strip. The strip may be politically connected to Arizona but geographically and historically it is more a part of Utah.

Mule deer browsing along the edge of the North Rim

Back in 1911, when Arizona was still a territory, Utah attempted to acquire the strip. However, the poet, travel writer, and Arizona historian Sharlot Hall, along with Flagstaff guide Allen Doyle, set out on a daring two-month-long

JOHN WESLEY POWELL

In 1861 an intense, largely self-taught, twenty-seven-year-old public school principal from Illinois joined the Union Army to fight against slavery. The next spring at Shiloh, as John Wesley Powell raised his right arm to signal a barrage, a Confederate minié ball shattered the bone in his forearm, requiring amputation. Undaunted, Powell continued to serve until almost the end of the Civil War. He then taught courses in botany, zoology, anatomy, entomology, and geology at Illinois Wesleyan University.

The summers of 1867 and 1868 were spent in the Rocky Mountains with his wife Emma and a small crew of students and relatives exploring and studying the upper reaches of the Colorado River. Powell hoped to "shed light on the central forces that formed the continent." This goal eventually led to a plan to explore a large blank area on the best maps of the time. He would descend the Green River to its junction with the Grand (note that years later, the state of Colorado had the Grand River's name changed to Colorado) and continue down the Colorado. He would flesh out terra incognito.

The nation's first transcontinental railroad had been completed recently, and Powell took advantage of the train to have four wooden boats of his design shipped to Green River Station, Wyoming Territory. On May 24, 1869, Powell and his nine-man crew of volunteers pushed off. Rapids quickly extracted their toll. A boat was lost, and one man left near Vernal, Utah. On August 10, they arrived at the mouth of the Little Colorado River and the beginning of the "Great Unknown." Little did they realize how difficult the rapids ahead would be. Endless days dragged on as the men toiled with the heavy boats, navigating what rapids they could, often lining or carrying the boats around un-runable cascades. Food was running short, and what they had left was moldy.

After three months on the river, they came upon yet another horrendous rapid—this time with no way to walk around. Three men had had enough of the river's challenges and of Powell's arrogant, aloof leadership. They hiked out through what is now called Separation Canyon and were never seen again. As it turned out, this was almost the last rapid. The next day, August 30, Powell and the remaining five men emerged from the Grand Canyon.

Powell's exploits made him a national hero. He would return to the river in 1871–72, better funded and with the previous trip's experience, to study the Grand Canyon region's geology and indigenous people. Powell went on to become a powerful bureaucrat in Washington, D.C., eventually becoming the second director of the U.S. Geological Survey and heading up the Smithsonian's Bureau of American Ethnology. He was also a founding member of the National Geographic Society.

1908 diagram showing expeditions along the Colorado River between 1540 and 1908

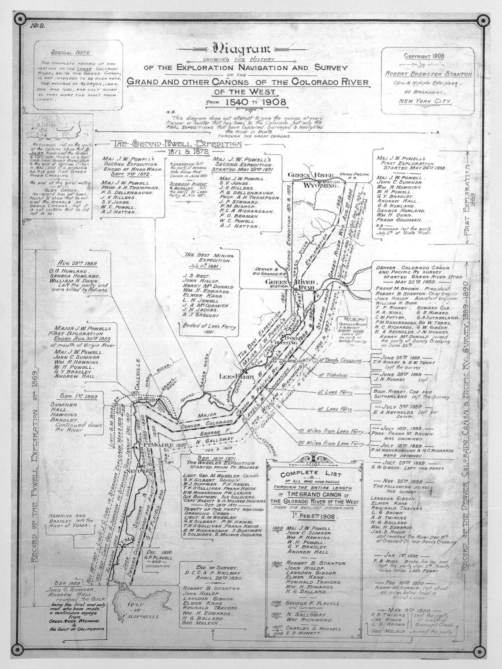

journey to explore the area, record its natural resources, talk to its residents, and chronicle its history. With two fine Arabian ponies drawing a Studebaker wagon, Hall and Doyle left from Flagstaff on July 23, and made their way north toward Tuba City and Lees Ferry on a dirt road that roughly paralleled today's U.S. Highway 89.

The road dropped down from the cool ponderosa pine forest into the warmer and drier pinyon–juniper woodland that was slowly replaced by grasslands, and finally entered the stark Painted Desert and Navajo country. It took them two days just to reach the banks of the Little Colorado River, which was in flood from summer thunderstorms. Fortunately, a mining outfit headed by Charles Spencer was also attempting to cross and helped them out.

Sharlot Hall and Al Doyle prepare to cross the Little Colorado River, 1911.

Hall and Doyle bought additional supplies at Preston's Trading Post in Tuba City before continuing north along the base of the Echo Cliffs, a route that dates back to prehistoric times as evidenced by petroglyphs and other artifacts scattered along the way. In the 1870s, Mormon pioneers upgraded this trail to a wagon road so that colonists from Utah could settle the valley of the Little Colorado River. Later, single men and women would return to Utah, usually to St. George, to be married in the Mormon temple and then enjoy their honeymoon on the trip back to Arizona. This route became known as the Honeymoon Trail.

The Echo Cliffs eventually angle toward the Colorado River and force travelers to seek a crossing. Hall and Doyle descended a dugway that . . .

15

The colorful sedimentary rock layers of the Echo Cliffs once covered the Grand Canyon region.

"... looked as if it had been cut out of the red clay mountains with a pocket knife; sometimes it hung out over the river so we seemed sliding into the muddy current and again the cliffs above hung over till one grew dizzy to look."

At the river bank was a board penciled with, "Fire a gun here if you want to cross." A little gasoline-powered boat ferried them across, and as Hall jumped out onto shore, she beamed, "... my Promised Land— in the 'Arizona Strip' at last."

Sharlot Hall on the North Rim, 1911

Upon her return, Hall wrote a series of articles extolling the importance of retaining the strip as an attribute of Arizona. The next year (1912), when the territory became a state, the strip was included.

This is big country. Take your time. Stop often and enjoy a part of America that has changed little from the days when Sharlot Hall explored it.

A NOTE OF CAUTION: If you decide to explore off the main, paved highways, go prepared. Take plenty of gas, food, and water. Cell phone reception is spotty at best. Tell someone where you are going and when you plan to return. Remember that these secondary roads can be impassable after rain or snow storms.

OPPOSITE:

Wotans Throne
at sunset

Part One
EXPLORING
the Grand Canyon's
North Rim

THE NORTH RIM:
GRAND CANYON
National Park

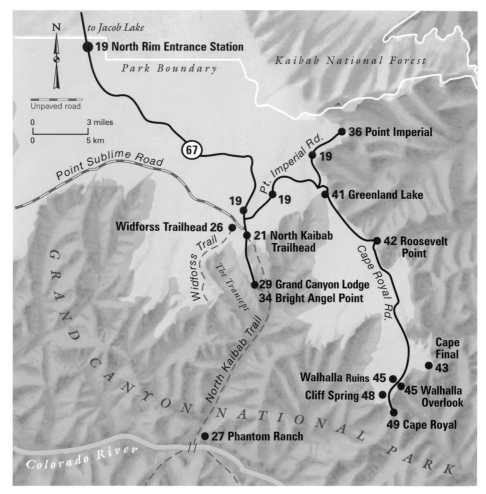

On February 20, 1893, President Benjamin Harrison set aside much of the canyon as the Grand Canyon Forest Reserve, but an 1897 law allowed grazing, mining, and lumbering to continue. After visiting the canyon in 1903, President Theodore Roosevelt felt that the area should remain pristine for future generations, and declared portions to be a federal game preserve on November 28, 1906. To further protect the canyon from uncontrolled development and use, Grand Canyon National Monument was established by presidential proclamation in 1908, again by Roosevelt. In 1919, Congress

Numbers on the map refer to page numbers for information about the area.

changed the monument's status to national park, and the United Nations Environmental, Scientific and Cultural Organization (UNESCO) recognized the canyon as a World Heritage Site in 1979.

NORTH RIM ENTRANCE STATION

From here it is 204 miles (328 km) by road to Grand Canyon Village located on the South Rim, though the North and South rims are separated by roughly 10 miles (16 km) as the raven flies. Immediately south of the entrance station is a long, narrow meadow lined with spruce and aspen trees, a great place to see deer in the early morning or late afternoon. The park road meanders south through Thompson Canyon to an intersection with Fuller Canyon, where a side road leads to viewpoints on the Walhalla Plateau. This part of the Kaibab Plateau was named by cartographer François Matthes in 1906 for the great hall of the Scandinavian gods, but prior to this time, Mormon cowboys called it Greenland Plateau.

OUTLET FIRE

Fire—exciting, dangerous, destructive, renewing. As you approach milepost 7 on Highway 67, and at many points along Point Imperial Road, you will see evidence of a forest recovering from fire.

Early managers of our forests viewed fire, whether human-caused or natural, as a destructive and wasteful event.

All means were used to prevent, detect, and extinguish fires.

And while it is still good advice to be careful with fire, forest ecologists and land managers have come to realize that fire is an important and necessary part of the natural ecosystem. Fire's exact role is still being unraveled, but certain aspects are understood. For example, in the spruce-fir forests of the North

Prescribed burns are used to improve the overall health of the forest.

Rim scientists believe that major natural fires may occur at intervals of up to 300 years, with less severe ones occurring every three decades on average. By contrast the more open ponderosa pine forests of northern Arizona have a frequent fire cycle of five to twenty-five years. Each vegetation type has its own unique fire ecology, which researchers are still trying

Stark tree skeletons in the aftermath of a wildfire

to understand. New research suggests that global warming may be contributing to an increase in the frequency and size of wildfires.

Active fire suppression has been practiced for nearly a century on the North Rim. Prior to that, livestock grazing, which began in the 1880s, indirectly lessened the spread of fires by reducing groundcover. But now forest managers are attempting to recreate more natural conditions. Prescribed burns are carefully and scientifically planned but are not risk free. They are an effective tool for mimicking lightning-caused fires, but sometimes the unexpected happens.

On May 10, 2000, just as the North Rim was opening for the tourist season, unexpected strong winds blew embers from a prescribed fire in Outlet Canyon, northwest of Grand Canyon Lodge, across the project boundary. The flames quickly swept east past Point Imperial and farther northeast to Saddle Mountain. Within twenty-four hours, the Outlet Fire had grown from 500 acres (202 hectares) to nearly 7,000. Roads were closed, visitors and employees evacuated, and almost 1,000 firefighters battled the blaze. By the time the fire was contained, more than 14,500 acres (5,868 hectares) had burned within the park and adjacent Kaibab National Forest.

Although, the burn covered more acreage than planned, it has provided fire managers and forest scientists an opportunity to study the effects of a large, severe fire within ponderosa pine, spruce-fir, and mixed conifer forests. Interestingly, there is no data to suggest that a fire similar to this one has ever occurred on the North Rim before. While much of the Outlet Fire was intense, in certain areas quaking aspen have sprouted with a vengeance. Within parts of the mixed conifer forest, aspen numbers doubled per acre on study plots where pre-fire data were available. The quantity of small aspens within the most intensely burned areas is astounding—4,000 to more than 15,000 stems per acre! How long it will take for the diverse mixed conifer forest to replace the aspens is unknown. (Read about the Warm Fire on page 56.)

NORTH KAIBAB TRAILHEAD

The North Kaibab Trail is the only regularly maintained trail leading from the North Rim to the Colorado River. But this is no casual stroll. It is 14 miles (22.5 km) one way to the Colorado River via Roaring Springs Canyon to its junction with Bright Angel Canyon. Shorter day hikes can be done to the Coconino Overlook (1.5 miles/2.4 km round-trip), Supai Tunnel (4 miles/6.4 km round-trip), and Roaring Springs (a strenuous 9.5-mile/15.3-km round-trip). Carry plenty of drinking water. And don't forget that it's a long, uphill climb back to the rim.

The 5-mile (8-km) round-trip Uncle Jim Trail, which is named after Jim Owens, also starts at the North Kaibab Trail parking lot and winds through the forest to a point overlooking the North Kaibab Trail switchbacks. Continuing from the Uncle Jim Trail along the rim to Point Imperial is the Ken Patrick Trail, where mountain lion spoor is not uncommon. It's about 10 miles (16 km) one way from the North Kaibab Trail parking area to Point Imperial.

The Uncle Jim Trail rambles through the forest over an undulating surface pockmarked with sinkholes. This is a topography known as *karst,* a term derived from similar geologic features in the Karst district of the Adriatic coast. Water seeping down through the Kaibab Formation has dissolved caves whose roofs occasionally collapse, forming circular sinkholes. Sinkholes may hold rainwater and become important water sources for wildlife. Also, the retention of moisture may encourage the growth of certain plants. Here on the Kaibab Plateau this may mean that aspen trees flourish in one spot while ponderosa pines are restricted to slightly drier zones.

The first topographic map of the Grand Canyon, arguably one of the finest maps ever made, was the masterpiece of François Emile Matthes, with the U.S. Geological Survey

(USGS). In the summer of 1902, he began mapping on the South Rim. When it was time to move to the North Rim, he was assured that Bright Angel Canyon was impassable. So Matthes and his men decided to use the rugged Bass Trail, about 20 miles (32 km) to the west. At the river, they discovered that Bass's boat was on the north side. Matthes and another man swam the dangerous river to retrieve the boat. Their horses and mules were reluctant to cross but were pushed into the water. The entire crossing took six days.

While mapping the buttes, mesas, and other formations of the Grand Canyon, Matthes opted to continue Clarence Dutton's tradition of applying "heroic nomenclature" to prominent features. He added names such as Krishna Shrine, Solomon Temple, Wotans Throne, and Walhalla Plateau to his map.

As summer waned and winter approached, the survey team decided to see if Bright Angel Canyon was indeed impassable. They were startled to encounter "two haggard men and a weary burro" emerging from the depths. Matthes and his crew roughed out a trail down Bright Angel Canyon to the river that was "so steep . . . that the animals fairly slid down on their haunches. So narrow between the rocks was it at one point that the larger packs could not pass through and had to be unloaded." They had to ford Bright Angel Creek ninety-four times. At the river, a prospector loaned them his boat for the crossing.

In 1903, prominent Kanab resident E. D. Woolley formed the Grand Canyon Transportation Company, which included a plan to provide a cross-canyon route for tourists. By 1906, Matthes's "trail" was improved by Woolley's son-in-law, David Rust, and his crew. The following year a cable with cage was strung across the Colorado River near the mouth of Bright Angel Creek. The cage, just big enough for one mule, was suspended from the cable on pulleys and pulled back and forth using a lighter cable.

Matthes mapping the Grand Canyon, 1904

Rust, described by an early client as having "clear-cut, regular features, and straightforward blue eyes," established a rustic tourist camp near the mouth of Bright Angel Creek. He dug irrigation ditches and planted cottonwoods and various fruit trees. After Theodore Roosevelt spent time here in 1913, on his way to the North Rim to hunt, Rust's Camp became known as Roosevelt's Camp. By 1922, Rust's old camp was superseded by the construction of Phantom Ranch, which offered comfortable cabins, a lodge, and a canteen.

EDDIE MCKEE

In 1964, geologist and former park naturalist Edwin McKee organized a Symposium on the Cenozoic Geology of the Colorado Plateau. The prosaic title gave little hint to the general public of what the scientists were up to. Basically, McKee and his cohorts were coming together to figure out how the Grand Canyon was formed.

McKee had a long association with the canyon. As a Boy Scout in Washington, D.C., his troop leader was François Matthes, who in 1902 had made the first topographic maps of the Grand Canyon. Twenty-five years later Matthes arranged for McKee (by then a geology student at the Naval Academy) to intern with paleontologist John C. Merriam, president of the Carnegie Institution of Washington D.C., who was developing programs for Grand Canyon National Park.

In February 1929, after park naturalist Glen Sturdevant drowned while attempting to cross the Colorado River, McKee was appointed in his place. At the canyon, McKee met and fell in love with a biologist named Barbara Hastings. However, there was literally a chasm between them. She worked on the North Rim, he was stationed on the South. But Eddie didn't let a 25-mile (40-km) hike one way interfere with his courting, and on the last day of 1929, they wed.

While McKee's 1964 symposium didn't answer the question of the Grand Canyon's origin, it did stimulate new theories and more research. The search for that answer continues today. Modern geologic science is only a few centuries old and is attempting to answer million-year-old mysteries. Just within the last three decades, major revelations in the nature of the earth's geologic functions have required new paradigms. The theory of plate tectonics has been proposed and widely accepted. The idea that contemporary river systems can evolve over time is being studied. And here at the Grand Canyon, new thinking has shown that the history of the rocks and the history of the river and its canyon have little to do with each other.

KAIBAB PLATEAU GEMS

KAIBAB SQUIRREL

A rare treat on the North Rim is to catch a glimpse of a Kaibab squirrel, a unique form of the tassel-eared group of tree squirrels. The Kaibab squirrel has a dark charcoal head and body, a rust patch on its back, and a striking, snow-white tail. This squirrel is native only to the Kaibab Plateau. (In the 1970s, the Arizona Game and Fish Department transplanted Kaibab squirrels to the limited ponderosa pine forests of the Uinkaret Mountains on the Arizona Strip.)

On the South Rim and beyond lives the Abert squirrel. It has a grey body with white underparts and a gray tail fringed with white. Both tassel-eared squirrels occur only where there are ponderosa pine forests, for they depend almost exclusively on that particular pine species for food and nest building.

The isolated population of uniquely colored Kaibab squirrels is an excellent example of what biologists call insular evolution. Islands, whether they are in the middle of the sea or biologically isolated land habitats, often have species that are endemic (restricted) to them. In this case, the "island" is the ponderosa pine forest of the Kaibab Plateau that is surrounded by desert.

How did the squirrels reach the plateau? One scenario suggests that before the Grand Canyon existed, the ancestors of these squirrels all lived in one huge, intact pine forest. As the Colorado River carved the canyon, the forest became fragmented and the resident squirrel populations became separated from each other. Over eons of time, the isolated North Rim population began to exhibit the dark body fur and white tail genes.

The problem with this theory is one of timing. Ponderosa pines probably did not spread into northern Arizona (presumably from the south) until a mere 10,000 to 11,000 years ago during the waning days of the last ice age. The Grand Canyon is at least several million years old. So, how did the pine trees make their way across the canyon, and how and when did the squirrel follow? So far, these are unsolved mysteries.

One thing known for certain is the important role these squirrels play in the health of ponderosa pine forests. Interwoven around the roots of the pines are specialized fungi. The fungi absorb water and minerals from the soil and produce growth stimulants, all of which are absorbed by the tree. The pine photo-synthesizes sugars for itself and the fungi in a classic symbiotic relationship. The fungi grow underground fruiting bodies called false truffles. But, how do the spores within the truffles get spread around to new pine seedlings? That's where the squirrels enter the story. Using their noses, they locate the false truffles (even under a foot of snow), dig them up, and eat with relish. The squirrels defecate on the run, spreading fungal spores through the forest as they go.

NORTHERN GOSHAWK

In spite of commercial logging since the 1920s and private cutting before then, the Kaibab Plateau still has the most extensive tracts of old-growth ponderosa pines remaining in the Southwest and the densest population of northern goshawks in North America. The Kaibab squirrel is one this bird's favorite meals. Since the squirrel is wholly dependent upon ponderosa pine for food and shelter, there exists a three-way relationship between the tree, the mammal, and the bird.

U.S. Forest Service researcher Richard Reynolds has studied goshawks on the Kaibab Plateau for more than sixteen years. His findings suggest that clumps of ponderosa pines interspersed with grassy areas not only make for ideal goshawk habitat but also provide perfect conditions for many other species. Reynolds believes that wildfire was the natural agent that maintained this type of forest structure. Unfortunately, overgrazing by livestock, fire, and heavy cutting of timber, especially old-growth trees, have upset this delicate balance. Reynolds hopes that his findings will help the U.S. Forest Service to manage the forest in a more ecologically sustainable way in the future.

FLOWERS THAT FLY

As you cross one of the lovely Kaibab Plateau meadows during the summer, you'll notice butterflies flitting from flower to flower in search of sweet nectar. Poet Robert Frost called them "flowers that fly, and all but sing." Entomologists have a general rule of thumb that says as you go from low to higher elevations, insect diversity decreases. But here at the Grand Canyon, diversity of butterflies and skippers increases with altitude. Additionally, there are four subspecies of butterflies endemic (restricted) to the park: scrub wood nymph (*Cercyonis sthenele damei*), Grand Canyon ringlet (*Coenonympha tullia furcae*), Kaibab swallowtail (*Papilio indra kaibabensis*) (below), and Schellbach's Atlantis fritillary (*Speyeria atlantis schellbachi*).

Incredibly, one of the greatest dangers to these unique insects is butterfly poachers. Delicate Kaibab swallowtails have been purchased on the black market for $400 a pair. Perhaps that doesn't seem like much of a problem, but consider that this same butterfly collector bragged about going into the Rocky Mountains and illegally collecting 20,000 butterflies on one trip! Then you begin to appreciate the serious impact of these unscrupulous collectors.

WIDFORSS TRAILHEAD AND
POINT SUBLIME ROAD

The Widforss Trailhead is only a quarter-mile (0.4 km) from Highway 67 on the Point Sublime Road, at the edge of Harvey Meadow. The meadow once served as a staging area for cross-canyon mule trips. The trail contours along the rim and around the head of The Transept on its way to Widforss Point (a 10-mile/16-km round-trip).

Gunnar Widforss sketching on the North Rim, circa 1934

Widforss Trail is named for Swedish-born watercolorist Gunnar Widforss. Widforss met Stephen Mather, first director of the fledgling National Park Service, in California while painting at Yosemite. Mather was impressed by what he saw and encouraged Widforss to specialize in painting the magnificent scenery preserved in national parks. His one-man exhibition in 1924 at the National Gallery of Art in Washington, D.C., included paintings of Yellowstone, Zion, Bryce, Yosemite, and the Grand Canyon.

Widforss remained a modest, self-effacing man un changed by broad recognition of his talent. From the early 1920s until his death on the South Rim in 1934, Widforss considered the Grand Canyon to be his home base. Unlike most painters, he did not restrict himself to the rim. "Weedy," as he was called by locals, often hiked into the canyon with his equipment to paint on site. At Phantom Ranch he might indulge in ranch manager Tom Moore's home brew, and on both rims he exchanged his paintings for room and board.

While representing the Church of Jesus Christ of Latter-day Saints (otherwise known as LDS or Mormons) in England, John W. Young, one of church leader Brigham Young's sons, conceived a scheme for turning the Kaibab Plateau into a hunting ground, including releasing African lions and Asian big-game animals, and making it a center for tourist recreation complete with hotels and lodges for English nobility. By coincidence, Buffalo Bill Cody was in England at the time with his Wild West Show and was persuaded by Young to come to the Kaibab and act as guide for two English lords, Colonel W. H. MacKinnon and Major St. John Mildmay.

The Cody party arrived at the South Rim in the summer of 1892. After being shown around by legendary prospector-turned-tour guide, John Hance, Cody and the prospective hunters followed a primitive trail around the eastern flank of the Grand Canyon and north to Lees Ferry, where they crossed the river and continued to the Kaibab Plateau.

PHANTOM RANCH

Architect Mary Colter was dynamic and authoritative—she had to be in order to succeed at a time when a woman in a "man's business" was still an oddity. Although Mary Colter's work is primarily along the South Rim, she did have the opportunity to design a rustic lodge and guest cabins along Bright Angel Creek in the canyon's Inner Gorge. Phantom Ranch replaced the ramshackle Roosevelt Camp, formerly known as Rust's Camp. After opening in November 1922, and until World War II, the ranch was a rather exclusive hideaway, attracting the wealthy and famous.

The ranch was expanded several times over the years. During 1927–28, eight guest cabins were constructed, the dining hall enlarged, and a recreation building added. During the Civilian Conservation Corps days of 1933–42, a naturalistic pond-shaped swimming pool was built. Water from Bright Angel Creek flowed in one end and out the other. (Unfortunately, new 1972 public hygiene regulations couldn't be met, and the pool was filled in.)

The CCC boys were stationed downstream of Phantom Ranch during the winter months; their campsite eventually became Bright Angel Campground. They built a spur trail to Upper Ribbon Falls and the 9-mile (14.5-km) trail to Clear Creek. A 1935 advertisement promoted a mule ride from Phantom Ranch to Clear Creek to enjoy the excellent fishing and visits to Indian ruins. The boys of Company 818 also constructed the River Trail that runs along the south side of the Colorado River to connect the Bright Angel and South Kaibab trails.

Beyond the Kaibab, the party visited Kanab, where they had dinner with Uncle Dee Woolley and his wife Emma. After the meal, Buffalo Bill praised Emma: "God bless the hands that made them custard pies." Though treated well, the British lords decided the plateau's game was too far from England and much too difficult to reach.

BRUCE AIKEN, ARTIST IN THE GRAND CANYON

Approaching Nankoweap, *oil on canvas, 40 x 36 inches, 2005*

As a child growing up among the concrete canyons of New York City, Bruce Aiken dreamed of living at the end of a long dirt road. Incredibly, his wish was realized in 1973 when he was hired to work and live at the Roaring Springs pump house deep within the canyon. For over thirty years, Aiken tended the machinery that pumped water to the North Rim. He and his wife Mary also managed to raise three children in this remote spot. Grocery shopping was sometimes a two-day affair. Other times, they just made do by baking bread, raising a small garden, collecting watercress for salad, and fishing in Bright Angel Creek.

Aiken is also an artist. As a teen, he trained at New York City's Art Students League and later at the School of Visual Arts in Manhattan. He initially found the Grand Canyon too overwhelming to capture on canvas; but as he studied and came to know his new home, he began to sketch, then paint small canvases. Slowly over time, he tackled larger and larger painting projects and is now recognized as one of the great artistic interpreters of the Grand Canyon and its many moods and secrets. After more than three decades of living below the rim, Bruce and Mary decided in 2006 that it was time to retire and seek new horizons. The pump house is now controlled by a computerized system.

The rugged dirt road continues past the Widforss trailhead to the westernmost viewpoint in the park, Point Sublime. But reaching it requires, at the very least, a high clearance vehicle and possibly four-wheel-drive. About 18 miles (29 km) one way, it may take two hours or longer in each direction. You can camp there with a backcountry camping permit. *Inquire about road conditions and possible closures before heading out.*

Bright Angel Point Area

ELIZABETH WYLIE MCKEE

Elizabeth Wylie McKee and her husband Thomas opened a tourist camp at Bright Angel Point in 1917. This was the first tourist facility on the North Rim. By this time, the South Rim was quite well developed with several hotels, including the fancy El Tovar, mule rides, and interpretive lectures. The Santa Fe Railroad had arrived at the South Rim in 1901, allowing visitors to reach the canyon in relative comfort. Reaching the North Rim was not so easy.

By contrast, earlier in 1917, Elizabeth's brothers Fred and Clinton became lost while attempting to reach Bright Angel Point in their Model T Roadster. They ran out of gas but were rescued by a sheep herder who eventually towed them back to town two weeks later.

Wylie Camp cabins, 1926

In spite of the difficulties, the Union Pacific Railroad envisioned building upscale tourist facilities at Bryce Canyon, Zion, and the North Rim. The railroad invited Elizabeth's father, William Wallace Wylie, to establish primitive camps at Zion and the North Rim as he had done in Yellowstone National Park. If these camps worked out, then the railroad would invest in resort accommodations.

William Wylie originated what became known as the "Wylie Way" camp concept. This consisted of a central services building surrounded by tent-cabins. The tent-cabins had wooden floors and walls to a height

Thomas and Elizabeth McKee (left), Wylie Camp proprietors from 1917 to 1926, with their son, camp workers, and Brighty the burro

of four feet (1.2 m), topped by three-foot (1-m) walls and roofs of striped canvas. The cabins were partitioned into several rooms, nicely furnished and heated with a Sibley Stove. Guided trips were offered and lectures and entertainment filled the evenings.

While William established a camp in Zion, his daughter and son-in-law went to the North Rim.

It was tough going. Firewood had to be collected and split. Water had to be hauled from a spring below the rim in Transept Canyon. Fortunately, a friendly gelded burro named Bright Angel helped with that task.

By 1926, North Rim visitation had increased to 14,500, and the camp showed promise of turning a good profit. However, the Union Pacific and the National Park Service decided it was now time for real development. The McKees were forced to sell out during the 1927 season as the Grand Canyon Lodge was being built, marking the end of the pioneer era of tourism at the North Rim. Although regional boosters repeatedly lobbied to get the railroad to build a line to the North Rim, Bryce, and Zion, the closest rail lines ever established were spurs to Marysvale and Cedar City, in Utah.

In the June 1921 issue of *National Geographic* magazine, geographer Harriet Chalmers Adams wrote,

> *"Here [at that time Roosevelt Camp, now Phantom Ranch] we discover the bridge mascot, Little Bright Angel, a gray burro who lives in Elysian Fields, with clear water, plenty of grass, and a care-free life. We fed him pancakes sent by the cook, his favorite dish.*

*"There are 113 crossings of the creek on the trail
up Bright Angel Canyon to the north rim, and
the little burro knows every one of them. Not long
ago he guided the foreman of the bridge-crew up
to the plateau, showing him just where to cross the
stream."*

Children's author Marguerite Henry wrote a number
of classic horse stories, but only one had a burro as the main
character. Newberry Award-winning *Brighty of the Grand
Canyon* was based on real people, animals, and events, including a fictionalized account of Teddy Roosevelt's 1913 cougar
hunt with Jim Owens. As Henry concludes, ". . . it is trail
dust out of the past, kicked up by Brighty himself, the roving
spirit of the Grand Canyon—forever wild, forever free."

GRAND CANYON LODGE

Grand Canyon Lodge seems to grow directly out of the canyon's
limestone rim. Early visitors typically arrived in a White Motor
Company bus, where college-age employees sang a welcome at
the entrance. Architect Gilbert Stanley Underwood designed
the rustic building so that visitors would be "surprised" by the
view of the Grand Canyon as they entered the front doors,
crossed the lobby, and descended into the Sun Room, which
faces the abyss.

However, the lodge seen today is not the original one
completed in 1928. The first lodge was commissioned by
the then-concessionaire to the North Rim, the Utah Parks
Company, a wholly owned subsidiary of the Union Pacific
Railroad. Stephen Mather, the first director of
the National Park Service, requested a rustic
design. Underwood's original
building included a massive

Spanish style exterior with a high front capped by an observation tower. A crew worked through the winter of 1927–28 to complete the lodge and its attendant cabins. The following summer, the lodge opened for business.

Tragically, in the early morning hours of September 1, 1932, a fire broke out below the kitchen and quickly spread. Within minutes the structure was engulfed in flames. The lodge manager, his wife, and the maids were able to escape the fire but watched helplessly as the building was razed. Fortunately, all but two of the nearby tourist cabins escaped the blaze.

The Utah Parks Company quickly erected a cafeteria and recreation hall but it was not until 1937 that a new lodge was completed atop the old one's foundation. The present lodge has sloped roofs for shedding heavy winter snows and no tower, but it retains the "surprise view" in the Sun Room.

Original Grand Canyon Lodge

The Sun Room provides a magnificent panoramic view.

The protagonist in Marguerite Henry's popular children's book Brighty of the Grand Canyon, *is immortalized in bronze by sculptor Peter Jepson.*

Soft, brown leather sofas invite you to rest and gaze through giant picture windows that frame a panoramic view of the canyon. This is also a wonderful, and safe, place to witness the fury of an afternoon thunderstorm sweeping across the gorge. In one corner a limestone-edged fireplace adds warmth and cheer on a cool summer evening or chilly autumn day. A statue of Brighty, the canyon's most famous burro and main character in the popular children's book *Brighty of the Grand Canyon*, is likely to be found nearby. The burro's metallic nose is polished bright by countless hands rubbing it for good luck.

The Colorado River is not visible from the lodge, but no matter. The scene unfolding at your feet is more than enough to inspire awe. And across the great gorge, beyond the South Rim, the horizon is studded with the numerous volcanoes and cinder cones of the San Francisco Volcanic Field, evidence of the area's more recent geologic activity.

BRIGHT ANGEL POINT TRAIL

Well-traveled tourist George Fraser remarked in 1916,

> *"I had been distinctly disappointed with the view from Grand View and the little we saw of the canyon from El Tovar [both on the South Rim]. The view from Bright Angel, though, proved fully up to recollection and expectation as affording an intimate panorama of the buttes, temples, and towers in the most crowded and characteristic part of the Kaibab division of the canyon."*

In the evening, take a short, quarter-mile (0.4-km) stroll from the Grand Canyon Lodge to Bright Angel Point, 8,148 feet (2,484 m) above sea level. Powell named the hidden creek below Bright Angel, after a character in Milton's *Paradise Lost*, to contrast with a muddy stream in Utah that he had christened Dirty Devil.

The light is softer now, the canyon's colors richer. Listen for the rush of water far below at Roaring Springs. This large spring provides all the potable water for both the North and

South rims. The inner, secret parts of the canyon are already in deep shadow. Deva, Brahma, and Zoroaster temples, all named by early geologist Clarence Dutton, glow in the waning light, and far to the south, the San Francisco Peaks oversee a phalanx of lesser volcanoes—some 600 in number. It is only 10 miles (16 km) as the raven flies to Grand Canyon Village on the South Rim. By trail the distance is 22 miles (35 km); by road the South Rim is more than 200 miles (322 km) away.

The views from the North Rim are both intimate and vast.

Silk-tassel bush, fragrant pinyons, gnarled junipers, and Gambel oak grow along the trail. The Kaibab Formation is spotted with chert nodules, crinoid stems, pieces of shell, and colorful lichens.

On a fall day, you may see across The Transept splashes of red Rocky Mountain maple, rust orange Gambel oak, and

yellow Utah serviceberry. Grey veils of rain are drawn across the wondrous space by cold zephyrs. Out of the dark, fuzzy clouds comes a sudden explosion of electricity followed immediately by the deafening thunderous rumble, which echoes and echoes off distant, obscured canyon walls. The rain turns to sleet. Winter is arriving on the North Rim. The last golden aspen leaves drift down to the forest floor forming a mosaic against wet, orange-colored pine needles. The wetness highlights the autumn colors, permanent coniferous greens, and smooth limestone. In the distance, passing clouds alternately hide and expose muted cliffs, temples, and buttes.

For an enjoyable stroll, the 3-mile (5 km) round-trip Transept Trail follows the canyon rim from Grand Canyon Lodge to the North Rim Campground. Also, a bridle path connects the Grand Canyon Lodge with the North Kaibab trailhead. This 1.2-mile (2-km) trail is open to bicycles, hikers, and pets on leash.

Point Imperial and Cape Royal Roads

POINT IMPERIAL

The highest viewpoint along the North Rim is Point Imperial, elevation 8,803 feet (2,683 m). The stunning panoramic view stretches from the Vermilion Cliffs to the Echo Cliffs and far into the Painted Desert. The dome-shaped mountain beyond the Echo Cliffs is Navajo Mountain, some 80 miles (129 km) away straddling the Utah-Arizona border. On an exceptionally clear day, the Henry Mountains can be seen 133 miles (214 km) away in southern Utah. In the foreground is the Coconino Sandstone monolith Mount Hayden, named after Charles Trumbull Hayden who arrived in Arizona on the first Butterfield Overland stage in 1857, and eventually established Hayden's Ferry on the Salt River, the site of today's town of Tempe, Arizona.

To your left, the major notch in the near ridge helps create the appropriately named Saddle Mountain. Also visible from here is the area where the Colorado River emerges from the relatively narrow gorge of Marble Canyon into the broad eastern Grand Canyon. The river is out of view but lies be the distant eastern rim.

Near the end of the last ice age, a Paleo-Indian hunter dropped his stone spear point in the Nankoweap basin below. Eleven thousand years later in 1993, an archaeologist discovered a fragment of this broken Folsom-style point.

For thousands of years, other hunters and gatherers traveled through this section of the Grand Canyon, leaving behind tantalizing bits of evidence— perhaps a split-twig figurine or enigmatic petroglyph. Beginning around 2,500 years ago, families built small, stone houses and began to plant maize in the Grand Canyon region. Twelve hundred years later, they grew cotton along with beans and squash, storing their harvest in granaries tucked into the cliffs. Hunting was still an important part of their lives, as well as gathering medicinal plants and wild foods when in season, such as pinyon nuts, cactus fruits, and grass seeds.

After several centuries of relatively stable living conditions, something caused the people to leave their canyon homes. Where did they go? Probably toward the east to become the ancestors of the Hopi and other Pueblo peoples.

The broken Folsom blade discovered in Nankoweap Canyon

Enigmatic petroglyphs (incised) and pictographs (painted) are occasionally seen along ancient trails.

More recently, other Native Americans came to live in the area, such as the Hualapai, Havasupai, and Southern Paiute, and later the Navajo.

The name Nankoweap may be derived from the Southern Paiute word *nengku'uipi*, meaning "land where people fought." This may refer to an incident in which Apache marauders from the south crossed the Colorado River, and ascended a route out of the canyon to the Big Saddle, where they surprised a camp of Kaibab Paiutes. The Apaches killed all but one of the Paiutes, a woman who escaped to "Indian Moccasin."

In November 1882, while "Encamped in snow, often concealed for days in the driving frozen mist and whirling snow," John Wesley Powell, director of the U.S. Geological Survey, and his crew "gradually overcame the apparently insurmountable obstacles" and improved an old Paiute route into Nankoweap Canyon. Once the trail into Nankoweap was completed, the eminent paleontologist Charles Doolittle Walcott and his assistants spent more than two months blazing a trail and studying the rocks along a major fault that runs west of, and is partly responsible for, the row of isolated buttes—Nankoweap, Kwagunt, and Chuar. The colorful, tilted rock layers (the Grand Canyon Supergroup) in this part of the canyon turned out to be much older than Walcott had suspected. He eventually reached the Unkar Creek area before retracing his steps back to the North Rim.

Not long afterward, horse thieves began to use Walcott's trail to connect with one on the south side of the Colorado, the Tanner Trail, to take stolen livestock from Utah into Arizona or New Mexico to be sold. Then horses stolen in those areas would be driven to Utah, again using these rugged trails. It was hardly an easy way to make a living. Not only were the trails long and arduous, but swimming across the unpredictable Colorado could be fatal.

Did these outlaws ever notice the seashell fragments in the Kaibab Formation? Did they puzzle over the animal tracks in the Coconino Sandstone? Did they see the impression left by an ancient fern frond in the Hermit Shale? As their horses kicked up dust between Nankoweap Butte and Nankoweap Mesa, did these trail-hardened men ponder the origin of the odd-shaped stromatolite fossils common in trailside Precambrian boulders? Or were they fooled by the gold-colored spheres of marcasite (iron pyrite) eroding out of the ancient rocks? Their thoughts and stories are lost to time.

In late October 1924, George McCormick, a prominent Flagstaff rancher (whom some have described as a horse thief), persuaded the regional forest service supervisor and the Arizona game warden to issue him a special permit to herd mule deer from the North Rim to the South Rim, where deer were relatively scarce. The state agreed to pay him $2.50 for each deer that made it to the south side and authorized him to move no less than 3,000 and no more than 8,000 head. Thirty to forty cowboys and rangers and about one hundred Navajo and Paiute Indians were hired to carry out the task.

On the afternoon of December 16, armed with tin cans, six-shooters, and cowbells, the men formed a line. With banging and yelling, the deer drive started along the lower eastern slopes of the Kaibab Plateau and slowly moved toward Saddle Mountain and the head of the Nankoweap Trail. With each step forward, the line wavered and became more disorganized. A threatening storm became a reality, and by the time the line

Little Colorado River Gorge

Marble Platform/Navajo Nation

Nankoweap Mesa

Nankoweap Creek

of men reached the rim of the Grand Canyon, ". . . there were no deer in front of the men but thousands of deer behind them." The project was abandoned.

During the Prohibition Era of the 1920s, illegal moonshine was transported along the horse thieves' route. Rangers discovered the remains of a still near Lava Creek, but thought this bootlegging site probably was older than the Volstead Act of 1919. As recently as 1937, horses were used on this trail, though one was lost over a cliff. After many years of neglect and erosion, it is difficult to imagine the Nankoweap Trail ever being suitable for horses. Today, it is not for the faint of heart or casual hiker.

For a less adventuresome trip, the excellent Ken Patrick Trail follows the rim about 10 miles (16 km) from Point Imperial to the North Kaibab Trail parking lot. The Point Imperial Trail, which is in poor condition as this book goes to press, follows the canyon rim northward through areas burned by the 2000 Outlet Fire. It leads about 2 miles (3.2 km) north to the park boundary. From there, you can connect to U.S. Forest Service roads and the Nankoweap trailhead.

Butte Fault

Kwagunt Butte

Confluence of Colorado and Little Colorado Rivers

Chuar Butte

Mt. Hayden

THE GREAT KAIBAB MULE DEER MYTH

After hunting mountain lions on the North Rim with game warden Jimmy Owens in 1913, Theodore Roosevelt remarked, "One important feature of his [Owens's] work is to keep down the larger beasts and birds of prey, the archenemies of the deer, mountain sheep, and grouse; and the most formidable among these foes of the harmless wildlife are the cougars." This prevailing attitude of the time ultimately tipped nature's balance between predators and prey on the Kaibab Plateau.

Within a few years of ceaselessly shooting, trapping, and poisoning coyotes, mountain lions, and wolves on the North Rim, hunters, forest managers, and visitors began to report that the Kaibab deer herd was exploding in numbers. A browse line became evident in the forest and forage was deteriorating. A movement to increase the number of hunting permits for deer became snarled in political maneuvering between state and federal officials.

Nature soon delivered her own brand of management. During the winter of 1924–25, thousands of deer starved to death and the population decline continued for a decade. From this "disaster," wildlife managers came to view the Kaibab deer herd as the archetype of ungulate irruption (a population explosion of deer) brought on by excessive predator control.

In recent years biologists have reexamined the Kaibab incident in light of new research into predator-prey relationships. Their findings indicate that earlier population figures are open to question, the increase in deer populations may not have been as dramatic as previously presented, and the lack of predators may have played only a small role in the drama. All that can be said for sure is that there was an apparent increase in the number of deer between 1914 and 1924, and that range forage deteriorated.

By the late 1880s, as many as 20,000 cows, 200,000 sheep, and unknown numbers of horses were grazing on the Kaibab Plateau. By 1906, through government regulation, livestock grazing had been significantly reduced. Did reduced livestock grazing allow vegetation to rebound, triggering an increase in deer populations?

Biologists believe that food supply is the major factor in determining prey populations. In turn, prey numbers influence predator populations. This is opposite the conventional wisdom of earlier wildlife managers. Predators, it appears, play a minor role in controlling prey densities. Studies conducted on the Kaibab Plateau indicate that lion predation, even at the highest rates measured, would not prevent deer herds from increasing provided there is adequate browse for the deer. Whatever the real dynamics might have been, the Kaibab deer story is an excellent example of how science, conservation, politics, and management interact.

Wouldn't Owens, Roosevelt, and other early sportsmen be surprised to know that the mountain lion is now viewed as a necessary spoke in the wheel of life? Hopefully, as our knowledge expands so will our wisdom to become better stewards.

GREENLAND LAKE AND SALT CABIN

Rain and snowmelt seeping through the porous limestone surface on which you stand can dissolve underlying stone to create sinkholes. Some of these sinkholes, such as Greenland Lake, accumulate enough silt and clay to make them somewhat impervious to water, thus creating a small pond.

This fairly reliable water source attracts wildlife and was used as a watering hole for cattle that once grazed the plateau. In the 1890s, Bar Z cattlemen erected the small cabin near the pond to store salt and other supplies.

The edge of the pond is fringed with sedges and tiny rushes, grass-like plants that favor the wet ground. Little gopher mounds of freshly tilled soil mark the lake's banks, but it's unlikely that you'll actually see the covert mammal. Pocket gophers spend most of their life underground digging elaborate tunnels. They have sturdy incisor teeth and long claws on their front feet, fur-lined cheek pouches, small eyes, and a nearly naked but highly sensitive tail. The tail acts as a "feeler" that allows the pocket gopher to run rapidly backward in the burrow.

Gopher eskers

Where the burrow nears the surface, a mound of dirt is thrown up. Usually, the gopher plugs its burrow opening to keep out predators like weasels and snakes. The tunnels are dug to the base of plants so that the roots can be eaten, and sometimes the leafy part of the plant is pulled below for a meal.

When the ground is covered by snow, gophers tunnel through the snow along the snow-ground interface to forage. Soil is pushed into these snow tunnels and when the snow melts, a network of earthen cores is visible on the surface.

ROOSEVELT POINT

On his first visit to the Grand Canyon in May 1903, Theodore Roosevelt instructed, "Leave it as it is. You cannot improve upon it. The ages have been at work on it, and man can only mar it." He declared the canyon a national monument in 1908, using authority granted in the recently passed Antiquities Act. Surprisingly, the man who was arguably most influential in helping to preserve the Grand Canyon didn't get a single feature named after him (except Roosevelt's Camp for a short time) until July 1996, when this point was dedicated by Secretary of the Interior Bruce Babbitt. Incidentally, it was President Roosevelt himself who extended to the United States Board on Geographic Names the authority to standardize, change, and assign geographic names.

After losing the 1912 presidential election to Woodrow Wilson, Roosevelt planned a hunting trip on the Kaibab Plateau that would include his sons Quentin and Archie, and nephew Nicholas. That trip would be followed by a pack trip to the recently "discovered" Rainbow Bridge near the foot of Navajo Mountain. Dave Rust, an outfitter from Kanab, would provide a guide, packer, cook, wrangler, pack outfit, and riding stock.

Nicholas was to make the arrangements. T. R. wrote to him to be sure to include ". . . 15 pounds coffee, some tea . . . ample supply of frijoles, some jerky, dried fruit (not prunes), thirty cans of sardines and a supply of Borden's condensed milk."

T. R., Archie, and Quentin arrived at the South Rim on the Santa Fe Railway's "California Limited." After spending the night of July 14, 1913, at El Tovar Hotel, the Roosevelt party climbed aboard Fred Harvey Company mules to descend the Bright Angel Trail to the Colorado River. Following

LEFT TO RIGHT:
Archibald Roosevelt,
Nicholas Roosevelt,
Theodore Roosevelt,
Jim Owens,
Quentin Roosevelt,
and Jesse Cummins

the Roosevelt Party down the trail was Henry S. Stephenson, manager of the Bar Z Ranch, one of the largest cattle operations on the Kaibab Plateau. As a July thunderstorm boomed above them, they took turns crossing the river in Rust's caged cable car, pulled slowly by an old man who turned out to be the foreman of the Bar Z.

Rust's cable car, circa 1910

But Rust's people were not there to meet them (they had the wrong meeting date), so T. R. decided to throw in with Stephenson and use his guide, the government hunter and game warden, Jim "Uncle Jimmy" Owens. Owens declared, "We'll eat off the land— mountain lion meat and wild horse flesh!" Although T. R. found Owens, a transplanted Texan, "to be diffident with a sad air, almost illiterate, he had the manners of a gentleman and was free from spite and malice." They spent two weeks hunting on the North Rim before continuing to northeastern Arizona to visit Rainbow Bridge, only the tenth party to do so since the natural bridge's discovery in 1909.

CAPE FINAL

It is about a 4-mile (6.5-km) round-trip hike from the dirt parking area to Cape Final. Geologist Clarence Dutton named this point in 1880. He wrote: "Point Final is doubtless the most interesting spot on the Kaibab. In pure grandeur, it is about the same as Point Sublime [but] the two differ much in the characteristics of the scenery."

Below this eastern edge of the Walhalla Plateau, the Grand Canyon Supergroup is magnificently exposed. These Precambrian sedimentary rocks are the remnants of ancient mountains. When these older Vishnu Mountains were worn down to almost a flat plain, a sea encroached upon the land, depositing the first layer of the Grand Canyon Supergroup. Simple, single-celled bacteria formed slimy mats on the shallow seafloor, mats that were preserved as stromatolite fossils in the Bass Limestone. Sea level fluctuated and other kinds of rocks were deposited: shale, sandstone, mudstone. Then lava began to ooze out over the landscape, in part caused by the collision of continents to form the supercontinent of Rodinia about 1,100 million (1.1 billion) years ago.

Another sea flooded the interior of Rodinia and more sediments were laid down. About 750 million years ago, Rodinia began to break apart. This spreading split the Grand Canyon region into blocks bounded by major faults or breaks in the earth's crust. Movements along these faults tilted the blocks into mountain ranges leaving the area looking much like modern Nevada with its uplifted mountain ranges separated by down-dropped basins or valleys. One of these huge faults is the Butte fault that runs roughly parallel to the east side of the Kaibab Plateau and west of the Colorado River. Much more recent movement along this fault is evidenced by several features. For example, notice that the far eastern rim, where the Navajo Nation is located, is several thousand feet lower than the Kaibab Plateau. Or, if you drove past Lees Ferry, recall how the land rises, climbing the East Kaibab monocline like a big wave as you drive west across House Rock Valley and up onto the Kaibab Plateau.

Erosion began to erase these ranges so that by 525 million years ago, the dawn of the Paleozoic Era, the area was once again fairly flat. Upon this landscape, another sea invaded. The Tapeats (a Southern Paiute word meaning "small rocks or pebbles") sands began to blanket the remnants of these mountains and the re-exposed Vishnu. This erosional contact, representing an incomprehensible amount of time missing from the rock record, would be named by John Wesley Powell the Great Unconformity.

The future Colorado Plateau (red dot) upon the supercontinent Rodinia 1.1 billion years ago (left) and 750 million years ago (right)

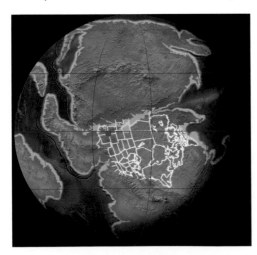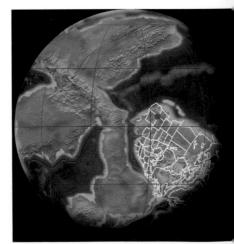

The limestone rim of the Grand Canyon was deposited 270 million years ago by one of many seas that covered the land.

But don't worry about understanding all the esoteric geologic details. Consider what naturalist John Burroughs eloquently wrote:

> "Time, geologic time, looks out at us from the rocks as from no other objects in the landscape. Geologic time! How the striking of the great clock, whose hours are millions of years, reverberates out of the abyss of the past.
>
> "Mountains fall and the foundations shift as if it beats out the moments of terrestrial history. Rocks have literally come down to us from aforeworld. The youth of the earth is in the soil and in the trees and verdure that springs from it; its age is in the rocks. . . . Even if we do not know our geology, there is something in the face of a cliff and in the look of a granite boulder that gives us pause."

WALHALLA OVERLOOK AND WALHALLA GLADES RUIN

Below you the long drainage of Unkar Creek meanders toward the Colorado River. The river sweeps around the edge of Unkar Delta, the site of one of the largest known prehistoric settlements within the Grand Canyon.

In 1949, Douglas W. Schwartz, a graduate student in archaeology, made his first visit to the Grand Canyon. He assumed, like other archaeologists of the time, that the inner canyon and the raging Colorado River were too inhospitable for large populations of prehistoric farmers. But thirty years of field work radically changed his thinking. After several archaeological surveys throughout the canyon, he and his crew conducted extensive pioneering excavations in three areas: Unkar Delta, Walhalla Plateau, and Bright Angel Pueblo, a small ruin along the Colorado River near the mouth of Bright Angel Creek.

From approximately AD 850 to AD 1200, the Ancestral Puebloan people lived on Unkar Delta and along Unkar Creek. There they grew corn, beans, and squash and built small stone houses to live in and kivas, underground rooms, for worship.

In the distance, beyond the Grand Canyon, are the Echo Cliffs and Painted Desert country. Much of that land is the Navajo Indian Reservation, but roughly in the middle sits the Hopi Reservation. The two groups couldn't be more disparate. The Navajo, or *Diné* (The People), are of Athapaskan origin, coming from Canada or Alaska through the Great Plains or Intermountain West and arriving in the Southwest probably no earlier than the fourteenth century. Traditionally, they were hunters and gatherers who did a little farming, lived in scattered family groups, and led semi-nomadic lives. On the other hand, the Hopi people are thought to be descendents, at least in part, of the Ancestral Puebloans whom the Hopi call *Hisatsinom* (a generic term for all Hopi ancestors). For millennia, the Hopi have been mainly agriculturalists who gathered together to live in villages.

The mouth of the Little Colorado River Gorge, a spectacular canyon in its own right, appears to the southeast entrenched in the Painted Desert. Up the gorge is the sacred Hopi Sipapu, a travertine dome formed by an artesian spring that bubbles with carbon dioxide gas and protects the entrance to their Underworld. Near the river's mouth are several small caves that drip with salt stalactites, a magical place where Hopi Indians ceremonially collect salt and leave behind tiny fetishes to become encrusted in the briny solution.

Behind you and across the road, a short path leads to the Walhalla Glades Ruin. This pueblo, excavated by Doug Schwartz and his crew, consisted of at least nine rooms and was occupied between AD 1100 and AD 1150. From this one small ruin, you probably wouldn't guess that the Walhalla Plateau was heavily occupied (seasonally) a thousand years ago. The majority of sites here are located along the edge of ridges overlooking drainages. Today's growing season is short, but when the Ancestral Puebloans were living here the summers were a little longer and wetter. Also, the Walhalla Plateau is somewhat warmer than much of the Kaibab Plateau because it juts out into the Grand Canyon and is washed by warm air rising from the canyon during the day. Past wetter periods may have meant lower temperatures, but the warm updrafts from the inner canyon would have helped mitigate those cooler temperatures.

Excavation of Unkar Delta

In this area the limestone is somewhat sandy and easily breaks into blocks and slabs that are useful for building structures. Chert inclusions offer a prime source of raw material for stone tools. Finely crafted axe heads were made for felling trees. By contrast, only poorly made axes have been found at Unkar. This is not surprising; the primary source of wood along the river was driftwood, hence there was no need for an ax. Water was probably always scarce on the plateau, but small springs and sinkhole ponds may have been more reliable than they are today.

Life was far from easy. The people were plagued with periodontal disease, tooth abscesses, and osteoarthritis. The dead were buried with pottery vessels and bracelets of shale and turquoise beads, possibly indicating belief in an afterlife.

CLIFF SPRING

The trail to Cliff Spring begins directly across from a small pullout located on a curve 0.3 miles (0.5 km) down the road from Cape Royal. The trail, a 1-mile (1.6-km) round-trip, descends a forested ravine and ends where a chest-high boulder rests under a large overhang. The tiny spring is on the cliff side of the boulder but may not be flowing. Drinking this water without purification is not recommended. This is often one of the better places to observe forest birds as they come in for a drink or to hunt for food.

Teddy Roosevelt and his 1913 hunting party camped here. Teddy's nephew Nicholas Roosevelt described the idyllic spot, ". . . turning a corner came in sight of an open gallery in the rocks . . . over which a ledge projected, making it a perfect shelter from all storms . . . near the end of it was a beautiful, clear spring, known as Cliff Spring, by which grew some enormous pine trees. . . . We made camp in what would have made an ideal robbers den in the Middle Ages."

Teddy Roosevelt in camp at Cliff Spring, 1913

CAPE ROYAL WOODLAND

The short walk out to Cape Royal passes very large cliffrose plants, which are a favorite browse of mule deer; Utah junipers, one of the more treelike junipers; big sage, especially aromatic after a rain; fragrant pinyon pine; wild currant; buffalo berry; Utah serviceberry; and fernbush, with its fernlike leaves. These are all plants typical of the pinyon-juniper woodland, a habitat typically found at a lower elevation. Warm, dry updrafts from the inner canyon apparently make this point of land too inhospitable for ponderosa, spruce, and fir found elsewhere at this elevation of nearly 8,000 feet (2,438 m).

Neat rows of peckings drilled into the trunks of pinyons and junipers by yellow-bellied sapsuckers are evident, and you may hear or see dark-eyed juncos (left), scrub jays, chickadees, or nuthatches (below). Uinta chipmunks and variegated

rock squirrels often come begging, but please do not feed them, or any other wildlife for that matter.

These isolated seeps and springs sometimes harbor unique plants and animals. During the last ice age when the region was much wetter, water-loving organisms were widespread. But as the Southwest became warmer and drier, only those individuals that could find a watery refuge survived and over time they evolved into endemic species or varieties. One such animal is the Kanab ambersnail.

This snail is known from only two locations—one is on private land near Kanab, Utah, and the other is Vaseys Paradise, a lush, verdant spring gushing out of a cave in the Redwall Limestone at the river's edge deep within Marble Canyon. Scientists have made several transplants to other canyon springs in hopes of increasing the snail's chances of survival against floodwaters periodically released by Glen Canyon Dam. These dime-sized mollusks are intermediary hosts for a rare parasitic flatworm. As the snails eat the damp vegetation, they ingest flatworm eggs. The eggs hatch inside the snail, where a single worm can grow to fill half of the snail's body cavity. The worm then pushes its neon-pink and green body through the snail's eye sockets and pulsates, which attracts the attention of birds. The birds feed on the snails and worms and excrete worm eggs.

Angels Window in morning light

CAPE ROYAL

Cape Royal was named in 1882 by Clarence Dutton who remarked that, it is a "congregation of wonderful structures, countless and vast, profound lateral chasms." An easy, paved, half-mile (0.8-km) round-trip walk takes you past Angels Window, a natural arch created by erosion along joints or vertical planes of weakness. The Kaibab Formation (and most other Grand Canyon formations) is fractured by many vertical cracks called joints. Joints may form when rocks are stressed, such as during uplift (remember, the Kaibab is a limestone formed millions of years ago in a warm, shallow sea and is now 7,000 feet/2,134 meters or more above sea level) or when the weight of overlying formations is removed (the Kaibab is Permian in age, and geologists presume that thousands of feet of younger layers once covered the region). Joints are further widened by the forces of erosion, such as freeze-thaw action. As two parallel joints erode, a relatively thin wall may result between the joints. This wall weathers thinner and thinner until one day a hole is worn all the way through and a window is born.

Continue out to Cape Royal, of which Roosevelt penned,

> *"From the southernmost point of this tableland the view of the canyon left the beholder solemn with the sense of awe. . . . The dawn and the evening twilight were brooding mysteries over the dusk of the abyss; night shrouded its immensity, but did not hide it."*

Have a seat, although the rough limestone blocks may require some padding. When geologists take in a landscape, two questions immediately come to mind. First, what is the origin of the various rock layers? Second, how did these deposits get shaped into the present landscape?

For the Grand Canyon, the answers to these two questions are long and complex and still being determined, at least the details are. But let's give it a go. We'll need to define a few geologic terms. There are three basic groups of rocks: metamorphic (formed under extreme heat and pressure), sedimentary (that's right, deposits of sediment), and igneous (born of fire, volcanic). Down by the river are the oldest rocks exposed in the Grand Canyon, although the range within that seemingly simple statement is astoundingly great. In this fairly open part of the canyon, the oldest exposed rocks are 1.2 billion years old. Just a few miles downstream, the river cuts into an older layer, the Vishnu Schist and related granites, that is nearly 1.8 billion years old.

San Francisco Peaks

Vishnu Temple

Those colorful, soft-looking slopes and ledges are the remnants of a mountain range that once covered northern Arizona. Sediments and lavas were laid down over millions of years until they accumulated to a depth of over 12,000 feet (3,658 m), more than two vertical miles (3.2 km)! Then these deposits were stretched (this was related to the splitting apart of a supercontinent—all part of plate tectonics, another fascinating topic), splitting along faults, then tilted into a huge mountain range. Enough time passed that these gigantic mountains were worn down until almost totally erased. Only remnants remained, such as what is seen below and in a few other places within Grand Canyon.

Eventually a sea encroached from the west drowning the region but also setting up the conditions for sands to be deposited near shore. Finer clays were carried farther out to sea and deposited; and in the clear, warm waters beyond that, corals began to grow. As the shoreline slowly shifted farther to the east, these three different depositional zones shifted eastward, too. Today we see the Tapeats Sandstone, Bright Angel Shale, and Muav Limestone as the products of this ancient Cambrian time.

The Cambrian sea retreated but another one encroached and the massive Redwall Limestone was the result. Environmental conditions changed again and again—more oceans,

Coronado Butte

Wotans Throne

desert sands, swampy periods punctuated by droughts, more seas. Millions upon millions of years passed. Then about 80 million years ago, the geologic story shifts once more from deposition to primarily erosion. The layers laid down during the Age of Dinosaurs, the Mesozoic, were carried away by water, wind, and time, leaving the Permian Kaibab Formation—the rough rock that you're sitting on—as the future rim of the Grand Canyon.

Oh yes, the Grand Canyon itself, that incomparable hole in the ground? This brings us to the second question: How did this magnificent landform come to be? The final answer is still being debated. The oversimplified explanation is this: The river did it. Geologists do agree that the river (or maybe more than one river) is responsible for the carving the depth of the Grand Canyon. The widening of the canyon can be explained by erosion and weathering of rocks by rain, freeze-thaw cycles, and chemical action. And gravity pulls all the fragments downward to the river. But the details, including the age of the canyon, are still being sorted out. The competing, evolving theories are excellently described in geologist Wayne Ranney's book *Carving Grand Canyon: Evidence, Theories, and Mystery.*

CLIMBING WOTANS THRONE

Wotans Throne was named by François Matthes while producing the first topographic map of the Grand Canyon. In 1937, a party of four men and a woman decided to challenge the mythological German deity by climbing his throne. A number of rappels were required to get down from the North Rim, followed by a climb of the formidable looking ridge to the summit of Wotan. They spent two nights below the rim of Cape Royal, one on the way and one on the return. One of the climbers, George Andrews, considered the feat more dangerous than climbs he had done in the Swiss Alps and Himalayas.

To their surprise, they found archaeological evidence that Native Americans had apparently lived on Wotans Throne. Why they chose such a difficult location for a home is still a mystery.

Part Two
APPROACHING
Grand Canyon's
North Rim

APPROACHING FROM THE NORTH:

JACOB LAKE
to the Park Entrance

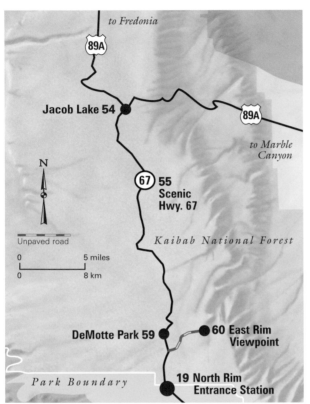

to Fredonia

89A

Jacob Lake 54

89A

to Marble Canyon

67 55
Scenic
Hwy. 67

N

Kaibab National Forest

Unpaved road

0   5 miles

0   8 km

DeMotte Park 59

60 East Rim
Viewpoint

Park Boundary

19 North Rim
Entrance Station

*Kaibab Plateau
Visitor Center*

*Numbers on
the map refer to
page numbers
for information
about the area.*

JACOB LAKE INN

In 1923, Harold and Nina Bowman, descendants of local pioneers, established a gas station along the old Grand Canyon Highway next to Jacob Lake, where "Fill 'er up!" meant siphoning petrol out of fifty-gallon barrels. Within a year they had built a small two-room cabin on a ridge overlooking the lake. In 1929, a new road was built that bypassed the lake, so the Bowmans relocated to the present site at the junction of U.S. Highway 89A and Arizona Highway 67. As you can see, their enterprise has grown considerably.

During the winter months Jacob Lake Inn serves as jumping-off point for snowmobilers, cross-country skiers, and snowshoe enthusiasts. Highway 67 south to the park entrance is closed to vehicles from the first heavy snow until spring snowmelt makes it passable again—usually mid-May.

Next to the Inn is the Kaibab Plateau Visitor Center, operated by the U.S. Forest Service and the Grand Canyon Association. This is a great place to acquire information, maps, books, and other material about the area.

About a 0.5-mile (0.8 km) south of the Jacob Lake Inn, turn west onto Forest Road 461 and drive 0.75 mile (1.2 km) to Jacob Lake (just a pond, even in wet years), named after Mormon scout Jacob Hamblin. Here you'll find the original

Jacob Lake ranger station built in 1910, only five years after the U.S. Forest Service was established. The cabin and barn are among the oldest forest service administrative buildings still in use today.

At the cabin you'll see blue and green mineralized rocks in a pedestal holding up an interpretive sign. This is azurite and malachite, copper carbonate ores, from nearby small deposits that were mined from the mid- to late 1880s. The ore was transported to Ryan (now abandoned), about 7 miles (11.3 km) west, to be smelted.

TOP: *Jacob Lake*
ABOVE: *restored ranger station at Jacob Lake*

SCENIC BYWAY: ARIZONA HIGHWAY 67

Anytime (providing the road is open!) is a lovely time to drive Arizona Highway 67, a 45-mile (72.4-km) Scenic Byway, from Jacob Lake Inn to the park entrance. But autumn is my favorite season. Aspen leaves have turned brilliant gold and the tree tops flame with color. The lower, wetter areas of the meadows abound with clover, mountain dandelions, wild daisies, sedges, and buttercups; at their drier perimeters buckwheat, pussytoes, cinquefoil, saxifrage, phlox, mountain parsley, and grasses are common. Purple lupine and red penstemon grace the shoulders of the road and a few New Mexican locusts still sport pink blooms. The flowering season comes late at this elevation (8,000 feet/2,450 m).

But don't hurry. Stop as often as possible at any the scenic turnouts along the road. Listen for the eerie, liquid, flutelike phrases sung by a hidden hermit thrush; look for a cautious bobcat creeping down to a sinkhole for a drink; admire the mule deer browsing at the edge of DeMotte Park; laugh at the antics of a rafter of wild turkeys stopping traffic as they gobble their way across the road; and be alert for the flash of a snowy white tail on the south end of a northbound Kaibab squirrel, or the sudden flush of the rare blue grouse.

It won't be long before you reach an area that has obviously been burned. On June 8, 2006, lightning ignited a fire about 14 miles (22.5 km) north of the Grand Canyon National Park boundary. For a week and a half, the Warm Fire burned at a low level of intensity, and the U.S. Forest Service considered

TOP TO BOTTOM:
Phlox; Quaking aspen bent by snowload; Bobcat

it useful in ridding the forest floor of accumulated pine duff, leaves, and dead branches. Also, burning some small trees and shrubs would help to open up the forest. Low-intensity fires return nutrients to the soil and increase growth of perennial grasses, forbs, and browse plants that, in turn, enhance wildlife habitat. They also reduce the potential for high-intensity fires that can destroy wildlife habitat.

Wild turkeys

On June 18, high winds from the southwest began to push the fire northeastward and suppression tactics were initiated, in part to protect buildings and structures at Jacob Lake. However, the fire's intensity dramatically increased during the evening of June 25. Fortunately, weather conditions began to change the next day; scattered rain showers fell on the 27th, but it took more than a week to contain the fire completely. By then 58,630 acres (23,728 hectares) had burned.

Some areas of highest-intensity burning occurred along Highway 67, turning once-lovely forests and meadows into devastated landscapes of gray and black ash. But about 65 percent (38,360 acres/15,524 hectares) of the area burned at low intensity, and rains later that summer already began to heal the forest. We may not like the way the burned areas look at the moment but remember that the long-term health of the forest ecosystem requires periodic fires.

PAULINE "POLLY" PATRAW: FIRST FEMALE RANGER-NATURALIST

PAULINE "POLLY" MEAD was a twenty-three-year-old botany student at the University of Chicago in 1927 when she made a summer-long field trip to the West, including a visit to the Grand Canyon. After setting up her camp in the Kaibab forest, her professor, Dr. Henry Cowles, suggested that she stroll through the trees and take a look at the canyon.

"I walked down the path and discovered the Grand Canyon. A most emotional experience. It was so wonderful." Later, as the group was leaving the Kaibab Plateau, Dr. Cowles pointed out how the trees came to the edge of a meadow and suddenly stopped. He wondered out loud why that was the case. Polly decided to investigate that question as her master's thesis. She spent the next two summers near the North Rim doing her research, which expanded into the first complete study of plant life on the Kaibab.

After graduation, Polly wanted to remain at the canyon. She applied for a job with the forest service but was informed that they didn't hire women. Then she applied with the National Park Service. Polly was sworn in on August 1, 1930, by the park's assistant superintendent Preston Patraw.

She was the first female ranger-naturalist at the Grand Canyon and only the second in the entire National Park Service. Since there was no official female ranger uniform, the superintendent decided that she should wear a riding habit topped off with "a hat like the courier girls for Fred Harvey tours wore."

A while later Patraw invited Polly to accompany him on a hike up Red Butte. Love bloomed in the spring of 1931, and they were married in May. Though Preston was transferred to several other parks, the Patraws ended up back at the Grand Canyon in 1954, when he was appointed superintendent. Polly had returned to her canyon home.

Why did the trees stop at the meadow's edge? Her answer was that the meadow soils were too high in lime content for the trees to thrive. Subsequent studies seem to indicate that the meadows are too wet in the spring for tree seedlings, causing them to rot, while hot, dry summer temperatures kill any that do manage to germinate. More recently, researchers have shown that the Kaibab Plateau's meadows have been decreasing in size since the mid-1930s but most dramatically since the 1970s, as aspens invade the meadow areas, perhaps due to fire suppression.

DEMOTTE PARK

While preparing for his second descent of the Colorado River through the Grand Canyon in 1872, John Wesley Powell

traveled from Kanab, Utah, to Big Spring, and on to the North Rim. He was accompanied by Professor Almon Harris Thompson and his wife Nellie, George Adair, two Indian guides, and Harvey C. DeMotte. While passing through this lovely meadow, Powell decided to name it after his friend DeMotte, a professor of mathematics at Wesleyan University in Illinois. The meadow is also called VT Park by the local cattlemen ("park" being a cowboy term for meadow and VT being a local brand).

What prevents trees from invading the meadows? One theory proposes that it has to do with the amount of soil moisture. Clay particles accumulate in low spots creating a barrier that prevents water

HISTORY ON BARK

As you hike through a gorgeous aspen grove, you may notice names, words, dates, pictures, and brands carved into their white-barked trunks. Archaeologists and historians have recorded nearly two hundred aspen dendroglyphs on the North Rim. Although scattered throughout the aspen stands, most are located along old roads or near water. They date from the 1890s to the 1950s. Many of the earliest carvings were made primarily by cowboys tending cattle during the short summer months. However, along the high Point Imperial Trail dates are mostly from December and January. Merle "Cowhide" Adams, a longtime cowboy on the Kaibab Plateau, cleared up the mystery. He recalled that after the autumn roundup, which moved cattle off the high plateau to the lower House Rock Valley, cowboys would return to "ride the points" after the first snowfall forced strays to the canyon rim. While these old carvings help piece together the history of the North Rim, it is considered very poor manners (not to mention illegal) to carve new ones.

from soaking into the ground. These relatively wet locations are not conducive to conifer sapling growth but do encourage grasses. However, since livestock grazing on the Kaibab Plateau began in the 1870s, trees, primarily aspens, have been able to slowly invade the meadows. The most dramatic encroachment has been since the 1970s, perhaps due to fire suppression.

EAST RIM VIEWPOINT

A 2.5-mile (4.02-km) graded road leads east from Highway 67 to the East Rim Viewpoint which offers an exquisite view of the Marble Platform and the northernmost section of the Grand Canyon.

From this point the broad Marble Platform spreads out before you, bordered on the north and east by the Vermilion and Echo cliffs, respectively. Lees Ferry is located to the northeast, where the two sets of cliffs almost come together. The huge gorge incised into the relatively flat Marble Platform is Marble Canyon, the upper reaches of the Grand Canyon. Zane Grey wrote, "The irregular ragged crack in

View from below East Rim Viewpoint

Vermilion Cliffs

Navajo Mountain

the plain, apparently only a thread of broken ground, was the Grand Cañon. How utterly remote, wild, grand, was that world of red and brown, purple pall, of vague outline."

Due east, squatting between the Echo Cliffs and Marble Canyon in that "purple pall," is the low flat-topped mesa known as Shinumo Altar. While mapping the Kaibab in 1872, Frederick Dellenbaugh spied the mesa. He noted,

> *"It stood up so like a great altar and, having in mind the house-building Amerinds who had formerly occupied the country, and whom the Pai Utes [sic] called Shinumo, I called it Shinumo Altar, the name it now bears. . . . It was the appearance that suggested the title, not any archaeological find."*

Several trails cross at the East Rim Viewpoint. Running parallel to the eastern edge of the Kaibab Plateau is the Arizona Trail (this segment is sometimes called the Kaibab Plateau Trail). The Arizona Trail starts at the Arizona-Utah border, continues south to meet the North Kaibab Trail, and, when completed, will offer a non-motorized corridor for the entire length of Arizona to the Mexican border.

Dropping down the East Kaibab monocline into the valley below is the North Canyon Trail. It's about 7 miles (11.3 km) in length and drops nearly 3,000 vertical feet (914 m) on its way through the Saddle Mountain Wilderness Area to House Rock Valley. The trail descends through mixed conifers and oak thickets into North Canyon and passes stands of old-growth aspen. The trail continues back and forth across a small perennial stream, where protected Apache trout have been introduced.

Shinumo Altar

ho Cliffs

APPROACHING FROM THE WEST:
COLORADO CITY
to Jacob Lake

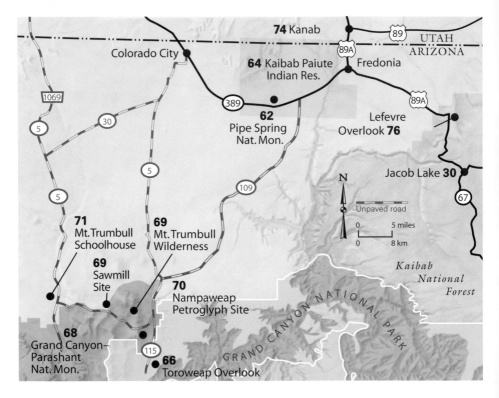

74 Kanab

Colorado City

64 Kaibab Paiute
Indian Res.

Fredonia

89 UTAH
ARIZONA

89A

389

62
Pipe Spring
Nat. Mon.

Lefevre
Overlook 76

89A

1069

5

30

5

109

N

Jacob Lake 30

67

Unpaved road

0   5 miles
0   8 km

5

71
Mt. Trumbull
Schoolhouse

69
Mt. Trumbull
Wilderness

Kaibab
National
Forest

69
Sawmill
Site

70
Nampaweap
Petroglyph Site

68
Grand Canyon–
Parashant
Nat. Mon.

115

66
Toroweap Overlook

GRAND CANYON NATIONAL PARK

This is big country with long vistas from the highway that can be deceptive. There is little indication of the deep canyons, dense woodlands, and jagged lava flows hidden beyond the pavement. Look across the plain and imagine ancient hunters stalking megafauna left over from the last ice age. Picture early people painting strange but wonderful images under overhangs and leaving animal figurines made of woven twigs in high, nearly inaccessible caves. Envision three of John Wesley Powell's crew members climbing out of the Grand Canyon only to disappear. It's a land made for legends . . . for imagination . . . for exploration and discovery.

Numbers on the map refer to page numbers for information about the area.

PIPE SPRING NATIONAL MONUMENT
On the vast, thirsty Arizona Strip, free-flowing Pipe Spring at the base of the Vermilion Cliffs has been a welcoming oasis for thousands of years. First, nomadic hunter-gatherers

depended on its waters; they were followed by Ancestral Puebloan farmers and, later, by the Kaibab Paiutes. Probably the first non-Indian to visit the spring was Antonio Armijo in the winter of 1829. With a pack train of mules, Armijo and his men were making their way from New Mexico to California along what would become know as the Old Spanish Trail (note that there were a number of variations to this trail).

About twenty years later, the Mormon Church instructed its members to spread out from the Salt Lake Valley to establish settlements in other parts of the Intermountain West. A few ranchers were drawn to the desert grasslands of the strip. In 1863, Dr. James Whitmore, a Mormon convert and cattleman from Texas, moved sheep and cattle to the Pipe Spring area. Whitmore and his herder Robert McIntyre built a dugout and corrals and planted an orchard and vineyard. Three years later, Navajos who had escaped capture by Kit Carson and the U.S. Army crossed the Colorado River to steal stock and ended up killing both men. Navajo raids continued on the southern Utah–northern Arizona frontier. In 1868, the Utah Militia built a small rock house at the spring, from which base they made one or two forays to keep the marauders southeast of the Colorado River.

Although the Navajo tribe had signed a peace treaty with the United States in 1868, they did not consider the Mormons to be U.S. citizens. Peace between the Navajos and Mormons finally came two years later when Jacob Hamblin and John Wesley Powell convened a peace talk between the Indians and the settlers.

John Wesley Powell and Paiute Chief Tau-Gu, circa 1873

Brigham Young purchased the ranch for the Mormon Church from Whitmore's widow. Young then called upon Anson Perry Winsor to manage it as a tithing ranch for the church. To safeguard Winsor and his family, two sandstone buildings facing a courtyard were constructed. Gates at each end of the courtyard enclosed the space and the main spring. A relay station for the Deseret Telegraph system was installed, connecting this remote outpost with other Mormon settlements, including Salt Lake City. Winsor Castle, as it became known, never saw an attack.

Church ownership lasted until 1895. The "castle" then passed through several

Winsor Castle at Pipe Spring National Monument

different owners and fell into disrepair. In 1923, Pipe Spring was designated a national monument by President Warren Harding and restored. Today the monument offers visitors a glimpse of Native American and western pioneer history. The Pipe Spring National Monument–Kaibab Band of Paiutes Visitor Center and Museum, operated jointly by the National Park Service and the Paiute Tribe, offers an opportunity to learn about the history and modern-day culture of the Kaibab Paiutes, their interactions with other tribes and cultures, and the movement of Mormon settlers into the area. Winsor Castle is fully restored and tours are conducted daily. Summer programs include ranger talks and costumed rangers demon-strating pioneer and Indian lifeways.

KAIBAB PAIUTE RESERVATION

Neung'we Tuvip is the homeland of the Kaibab Paiutes. It stretches from the Grand Canyon on the south to the north-east drainages of the Virgin River on the north, and from Kanab Canyon on the west to the Paria River on the east. Their territory ranges in elevation from about 2,000 feet (610 m) at the Colorado River to over 9,000 feet (2,743 m) on the Kaibab Plateau, thus covering a wide range of natu-ral habitats containing many different resources for survival. The many sacred sites across the Arizona Strip and within the Grand Canyon are monitored by tribal members.

According to the Kaibab Paiutes, their ancestors were the *E'nengweng*. This is the prehistoric culture that archaeologists have termed Anasazi or, more recently, Ancestral Puebloan. Archaeologists generally believe that the earlier people left before the Kaibab Paiute ancestors arrived about AD 1100. The Kaibab Paiutes believe that the scattered panels of ancient *tumpee'po'ohp* (pictographs and petroglyphs) are a sacred link to their ancestors.

Traditionally, the Southern Paiutes moved seasonally through their territory to take advantage of ripening fruits and seeds and to hunt deer, bighorn sheep, and other animals. They built conical brush and branch shelters called *kahn* for sleeping and protection from inclement weather. As the dominant culture of the twentieth century encroached upon them, traditional living proved to be more and more difficult.

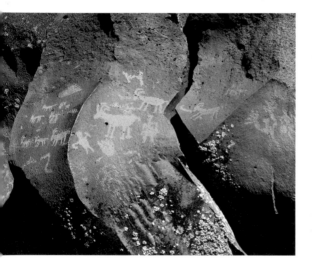

Petroglyphs often include images of bighorn sheep

Tragically, by 1873 the majority of the Kaibab band was dead from disease, war, and starvation. Paiutes depended greatly on gathering grass seeds to grind into meal; however, overgrazing by pioneer livestock had decimated the grasslands by the 1880s. Their neighboring relatives, the Shivwits, Kaiparowits, and Uinkaret paiutes, were forced off the Arizona Strip in 1891 and relocated to reservations in southwest Utah.

The Kaibab Paiutes were granted a reservation of their own in 1907. Some became cattle ranchers and others worked for local white settlers. Local ranchers continued to use much of the reservation land until a federal lawsuit removed them in 1925.

From 1994 to 1996 the Kaibab Paiutes ran a small gambling casino on their land, but its proximity to Las Vegas kept it from being very profitable. Today, the tribe operates a convenience store and gas station, along with an RV park and campground. Some tribal members work at Pipe Spring National Monument, which is located within the reservation. Although not an easy task, they are dedicated to preserving their culture and language.

DETOUR TO TOROWEAP OVERLOOK

Sixty miles (96.5 km) south of Pipe Spring, across Tuweep Valley, is Toroweap Overlook, an icon of western Grand Canyon frequented by landscape photographers and geologists but seldom visited by the average tourist. The view at the end of the dirt road makes the trip worthwhile for those who are well equipped. There are no services and cell-phone coverage is spotty, at best. Allow at least two hours each way to traverse the bone-jarring dirt road. A high-clearance vehicle is recommended.

One translation of Toroweap is "deep gorge." The Grand Canyon is quite narrow at this point and drops approximately 3,000 vertical feet (900 m) to the Colorado River. Downstream you can see and hear Lava Falls. Though it looks like a riffle from the rim, it is one of the most treacherous of the Colorado's rapids.

When explorer John Wesley Powell encountered Lava Falls, he exclaimed, "What a conflict of water and fire there must have been here! Just imagine a river of molten rock running down in to a river of melted snow. What a seething and boiling of the waters; what clouds of steam rolled into the heavens!"

Although Vulcans Throne, a cinder cone, sits prominently on the canyon rim above the rapids, the black lava cascading down the canyon wall came from cones farther north on the western edge of Tuweep Valley, beginning approximately 630,000 years ago. These flows created lava dams across the Colorado River that were eventually filled to capacity, overflowed, and eroded once again by the power of running water. Remnants of these dams (one of which was over 2,000 feet/610 meters high) are visible as horizontal layers of basalt at the base of the cascades. However, the rapids seen today are not the remnants of these igneous dams. Rather, debris flows and flash floods have washed boulders and sediment out of Prospect Canyon, constricting the river and forming the rapids. Debris flows are floods consisting of sediment and water that typically contain more then 80 percent solids. These sediments can range from fine clay particles to extraordinarily huge boulders—one of which measured in a 1990 debris flow weighed an estimated 290 tons (263,000 kilos).

In 1995 a research team was camped near the mouth of Prospect Canyon studying past debris flows when a tremendous rain storm hit during the night. They were startled to hear a roaring sound that they interpreted as a signal that the Colorado River was rising from accumulated storm runoff. But after a few minutes the noise subsided. In the morning they discovered that a new debris fan coming out of Prospect Canyon was constricting part of the Colorado River at Lava Falls Rapid, creating monstrous waves and trapping them above an unrunable rapid. The river promptly began to erode away the edge of the debris fan, and by afternoon a navigable passage through Lava Falls developed. The scientists were able to determine that this 1995 debris flow was the third largest to occur at his location in the past 100 years—a remarkable thing to witness.

One person comes to mind when speaking of Toroweap country—Ranger John

Riffey. Riffey was one of those rare, remarkable individuals who relished remote places but also was affable and friendly to a fault. Unlike many park service rangers who transfer from park to  park throughout their careers, Riffey steadfastly manned his post in the Tuweep Valley for nearly forty years.

When he was first assigned to this outpost at Grand Canyon National Monument in 1942, it was his job to make sure that overgrazing did not occur within the monument, where some preexisting grazing leases were "grandfathered in" when the monument was established. In the early days, it was an all-day drive to the nearest town of Kanab. But Riffey learned to fly his own airplane, a Super Cub, which he christened Pogo. He nicknamed most of the park service equipment, too. George was the barometer; Matilda was the front-end loader; Sparky, of course, was the generator; and Big Scratchy was the road grader. Whether it was getting directions to the Lava Falls Trail or munching on homemade chocolate chip cookies, all who met Riffey and his wife, fervent ornithologist Meribeth, remember their kindness and good cheer. They're both gone now, but they are laid to rest not far from their beloved Grand Canyon home.

This isolated part of the park was first established as Grand Canyon National Monument by President Herbert Hoover in 1932. In spite of its inaccessibility, annual visitation at Toroweap reached 1,000 by the 1960s, and it was officially added to the park as part of the Grand Canyon Enlargement Act in 1975.

There is a campground near Toroweap Overlook. "At Large" camping in the backcountry requires a permit from the park's Backcountry Office (see Appendix B, page 93).

ABOVE: *Vulcans Throne and lava cascades*

VENTURING OFF PAVEMENT: A WARNING!

While there are many sites on the remote Arizona Strip that are worth exploring, do not leave the paved highway unless you are sure that the roads are passable and you have appropriate maps (available at forest service and Bureau of Land Management visitor centers). High-clearance vehicles with two full-size spare tires are strongly recommended. There are no services once you leave the pavement of Highway 389. Cell phone reception is spotty at best, nonexistent at worst.

GRAND CANYON–PARASHANT
NATIONAL MONUMENT

CAUTION: You must have appropriate maps to find your way around the monument. Maps are available at forest service and Bureau of Land Management visitor centers. There are

Parashant Canyon

no paved roads or visitor services within the monument's million-plus acres (0.4 million hectares).

In 2000, President Bill Clinton signed a proclamation setting aside over 1 million acres (0.4 million hectares) of the southwestern portion of the Arizona Strip as the Grand Canyon–Parashant National Monument. This monument encompasses several designated wilderness areas, part of Lake Mead National Recreation Area, and vast acreage of wilderness and important wildlife habitat on the Uinkaret and Shivwits plateaus and along the Grand Wash Cliffs.

The Uinkaret Plateau is punctuated by a series of volcanoes: mounts Trumbull, Emma, Logan, and Petty Knoll. In between are more than a hundred smaller cinder cones and basaltic lava flows. Its east flank is delineated by Toroweap Valley, whereas its west side drops off along a major fault that has created the Hurricane Cliffs. Powell recorded that the Southern Paiute called this plateau Uinkaret meaning "ponderosa pine trees sitting" or "place of the pines."

MOUNT TRUMBULL WILDERNESS

Mount Trumbull, the highest peak in the Uinkaret Mountains at 8,000 feet (2,441 m), is a shield volcano, meaning that it resembles a shield in profile. This type of volcano is formed by successive layers of basalt building up a mountain with moderately-angled sloping sides. The mountain was named by Powell in 1870 for Illinois Senator Lyman Trumbull, who helped Powell obtain funds for his first Colorado River expedition. Nearby Mount Emma is named after Trumbull's wife.

SAWMILL SITE & TEMPLE TRAIL

Between the early 1870s and 1940s, numerous owners and managers operated a series of sawmills on the Arizona Strip. The first one was here at the base of Mount Trumbull and it provided timbers and lumber for the construction of the Mormon Temple in St. George, Utah, which was dedicated in 1877. The wood was hauled in wagons pulled by oxen some 80 miles (129 km) to St. George over a rough road known as the Temple Trail.

Adjacent to the sawmill site, but not very apparent, is

Sawmills existed on Mt. Trumbull at various times and locations to harvest stands of ponderosa pine trees. They produced the lumber for the Church of Jesus Christ of Latter-day Saints temple in St. George, Utah. The trail from the sawmills on Mt. Trumbull to the temple site in St. George became known as the Temple Trail. Huge timbers were cut, loaded on wagons, and pulled by horses and mules over the narrow, twisted, and rocky 66-mile jouney.

the Uinkaret Pueblo, a prehistoric Ancestral Puebloan site now marked by just a few lines of basalt rocks. Unfortunately, the site has been pothunted. Please do not disturb it further.

NAMPAWEAP PETROGLYPH SITE

GETTING THERE: This site is accessed by way of the Mount Trumbull Road about 3 miles (4.8 km) east of the Mount Trumbull trailhead and 3.5 miles (5.6 km) west of the Toroweap/Tuweep road. Drive south 1.1 miles (1.8 km) and then turn east to the parking lot on your right. Park here and walk 0.75 mile (1.2 km) down the trail to the head of Nampaweap Canyon.

Nampaweap, derived from the Paiute words *Nampaya Uip* meaning "foot canyon," contains hundreds of petroglyphs carved into the basalt cliffs and boulders in this small canyon. The petroglyphs date from Archaic to Paiute times. This drainage was probably an important prehistoric route between the Grand Canyon and the resources of the ponderosa pine forests around Mount Trumbull. The predominance of bighorn sheep glyphs led local cowboys to call the place Billy Goat Canyon.

MOUNT TRUMBULL SCHOOLHOUSE

GETTING THERE: To reach the schoolhouse and the former town site, take Quail Hill Road (BLM Road 1069) to Main Street Valley Road (County Road 5). Go prepared. There are no facilities.

Homesteaders began to settle this remote part of the Arizona Strip around 1916. One homesteader, Abraham Bundy, arrived after being forced out of Mexico by Pancho Villa. His family officially named their tiny community Mount Trumbull after the nearby volcano, but most locals called it Bundyville. By the 1930s, there were about 250 people living in the area. They dry-farmed corn, beans, wheat, squash, and other crops for their own consumption and to sell in distant towns such as St. George, Utah. But making a living was tough. Place names like Poverty Mountain, Hungry Valley, Last Chance Spring, and Death Valley attest to the rough life of these pioneers.

It is roughly 60 miles (96.5 km) to St. George from here, and until the 1920s the trip was made by horse and wagon. Drought in the 1930s made farming more difficult, and after the passage of the Taylor Grazing Act of 1934, most residents started sheep or cattle ranches. Although a few hardy souls continue to live in the area, by the 1960s most had moved away from Mount Trumbull into the towns of Washington County, Utah, and Fredonia, Arizona.

Mt. Trumbull schoolhouse before fire and after restoration, 1967

The old Mount Trumbull schoolhouse, built in 1918, served many functions besides "learnin' the three Rs." It also functioned as a church, dance hall, and town meeting house. People came from miles around to attend dances, which was a main source of entertainment. The local population declined, and the school was closed in 1966.

Lumber for the school came from the pine forest to the east and was dragged by horse-drawn wagons down the Old Slide Road, so called because it was so steep that the wagon wheels had to be locked and the wagon skidded down the incline.

BURRO BILL AND ME

In early 1934, in the depths of the Great Depression, Burro Bill Price and his wife Edna left their home and trading post in Death Valley, California, bought three-months worth of supplies in Mesquite, Nevada, and headed out across the Arizona Strip with their string of burros. They had decided that Death Valley had become too tame and were searching for wild country. At St. Thomas, a small town that was destined to be submerged by the new lake that was forming behind Hoover Dam, the few remaining residents warned them, "That Strip ain't healthy. People live over there that dassent come out. Might be you and your burros'll end up over a cliff. Better stay outa there." But the Prices weren't easily dissuaded.

When they reached the strip, they discovered that Arizona was in the midst of a terrible drought. The few ranchers that remained were quickly losing their livestock to starvation and thirst. They met a friendly, moonshining hermit who also rustled a few cows on the side, heard about a cave full of human bones, and ran into some unsavory characters hiding out from the law.

As Bill and Edna walked down the dusty streets of Bundyville (Mount Trumbull), they passed one bright young woman surrounded by five small children clamoring to see the donkeys. The Prices asked where they could get a drink for themselves and their animals. The woman replied that there was only a little left, but they were welcome to it, for "the town is moving tomorrow. Any place we can get water."

After some time spent in this remote Mormon village, Edna noted, "Everywhere we went, there were women and children in an amazing ratio, but nowhere did we see any men. . . . These were an earthy, humorous people, shrewd in business, clannish but tolerant, forgiving, letting each man tend to his own salvation." Most of the town's men were working at the sawmill on the slopes of Mount Trumbull.

Continuing their journey eastward, they encountered irritable, armed cattlemen guarding "their" springs from the "blasted polygamous nesters" (the Mormons) and Ozark Jim White, a friendly giant of a man, who lived with ". . . six ragged cats, seven yellow dogs, three little mules, a flock of hens and fifty goats." To circumnavigate the enormous Kanab Canyon, they headed north to Pipe Spring National Monument. Once there, they took part in the spring roundup to make a little money and to resupply their meager larder. Burro Bill, never one to turn down anything anybody else would eat, tried the "mountain oysters." Edna stuck with cowboy beans.

Poverty Mountain

Grassy Mountain

Mt. Dellenbai

They left the hot, dry desert lowlands of the strip and climbed into the cool forest of the Kaibab Plateau, where they spent the summer poaching a couple of deer for jerky (with a wink and a nod from a understanding ranger) and enjoying the wild beauty of the area. As winter approached, they gathered their burros and went into the Grand Canyon following the North Kaibab Trail, crossed the Colorado River on the bridge (no mean feat considering the irascibility of burros) and ascended to the South Rim to continue south in search of new adventures in the quickly disappearing wild places of the Southwest.

In 2000 vandals torched the historic building but descendants of the first families, in cooperation with the Bureau of Land Management (BLM), have built a replica.

SHIVWITS PLATEAU

The westernmost of the six Arizona Strip plateaus is the Shivwits, bounded on the east by the Hurricane Cliffs and on the west by the giant steps of the Grand Wash Cliffs. Only a few small mountains—Poverty Knoll, Poverty Mountain, Grassy Mountain, and Mount Dellenbaugh—relieve the relatively flat topography of the Shivwits. Of those, Frederick Dellenbaugh, who at seventeen years of age had been the youngest member on Powell's second Colorado River trip in 1871, unabashedly boasted that the mountain Powell named for him was one of the finest in the Southwest. In reality it was only a modest volcanic hill.

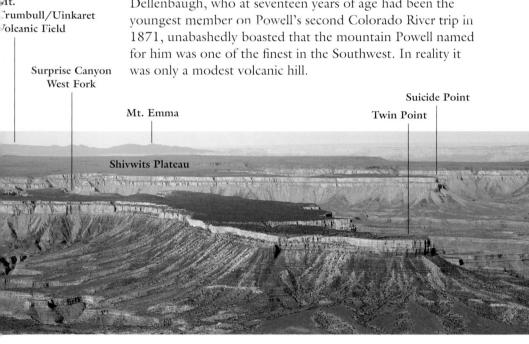

Mt. Trumbull/Uinkaret Volcanic Field

Surprise Canyon West Fork

Mt. Emma

Shivwits Plateau

Suicide Point

Twin Point

A mystery persists in the Shivwits Plateau area as to what became of the three men who abandoned Powell's 1869 exploratory river trip. William Dunn and Oramel and Seneca Howland left the river to climb out of the Grand Canyon to the north toward the Mormon settlements. Amazingly, the side canyon that they traveled up, now called Separation Canyon, was one of the few that offered passage to the rim. Presumably, they made it at least as far as Mount Dellenbaugh, where a boulder on its upper slopes has Dunn's inscription plus the word "water" and an arrow pointing north.

Not long after the successful completion of Powell's river journey, the *Deseret Evening News* reported that the three men had been killed by Indians. Once Powell was back in the East, he received a telegraph message relaying this information, but did not investigate further at that time.

The following year, Powell spent six days exploring the strip with the help of Mormon scout Jacob Hamblin in hopes of learning more about the men's disappearance. Powell and Hamblin encountered a band of Shivwits Paiutes, and with the scout translating, the Indians supposedly confessed to killing the three white men. The Indians claimed that they had mistaken them for several drunken prospectors who had killed a woman from a neighboring tribe. And that became the official historical record.

But in the 1980s, rumors began to circulate that the Indians were not the culprits. Instead, Powell's three men had encountered some Mormons who believed they were federal government spies. At this time Mormon suspicion was rampant and emotions ran high, especially in southern Utah, because of the U.S. government's intervention in Utah Territory's affairs—in part because of the massacre of immigrant families at Mountain Meadows in 1857 (see page 83).

This revision of history purports that the three men were taken to the tiny hamlet of Toquerville, Utah, near Zion National Park. For an unknown reason, they were killed, and the people involved in the murder swore one another to secrecy. Although, this story has spread among river guides and others as gospel, more recent research casts doubt on its veracity. If you are curious, see Don Lago's article in the Grand Canyon River Guides' *Boatman's Quarterly Review* (Fall 2003, Volume 16, Number 3).

In the remote Surprise Canyon that cuts into the Shivwits Plateau, biologists have discovered what may turn out to be a new species of leopard frog. Leopard frogs of various species once occurred in a number of springs, streams, and riparian zones on the Colorado Plateau but are now either scarce or entirely gone from former habitats. The reasons for this are still unclear.

FREDONIA TO KANAB

From Fredonia, Arizona, a short 7-mile (11.3-km) detour north on U.S. Highway 89A brings you to Kanab, Utah. Halfway in between is the Arizona-Utah border on the 37th Parallel, the exact location of which was fixed by the Powell Survey during their 1871–72 winter survey.

According to an old cowboy by the name of Rowland

Rider, it was here on the border that a little saloon was constructed back in the 1890s. It was a two-room affair, with a bar at one end and the barkeeper's bedroom at the other. The entire building sat on top of log rollers. Not surprisingly, this establishment was very popular with the local cowboys. Their wives, however, were none too happy. One day the women in Kanab decided that while their husbands were off working, they would torch the saloon.

By chance, the saloon keeper saw the angry wives coming and rolled the building across the state line into Arizona. As the women readied their torches, he admonished them, "You can't touch this business; it's in Arizona." Upon which, the women went back home in disgust.

Rowland Rider at a rodeo in Kanab, 1912

Later, the wives in Fredonia got fed up with their husbands' drinking and came riding down on the saloon. Again, the saloon keeper saw them coming and pushed the bar into Utah. This back-and-forth rolling of the saloon went on for years . . . at least, according to old cowboy Rider.

Rowland Rider was a full-time wrangler on the strip from 1907 until 1910, then cowboyed for a few more years just during the summers. In 1919 he returned and served as marshal of Kanab until he moved to Salt Lake City in 1928.

UNCLE DEE WOOLLEY

One of the early promoters of the North Rim was Edwin Dilworth "Uncle Dee" Woolley, described as having "an Irish cast countenance, clean shaven, stockily built." He and his nephew Gordon sponsored the first attempt to drive an automobile from Salt Lake City via Kanah to the North Rim. In June 1909, a Locomobile and a Thomas Flyer made the journey from Kanab in three days. Gasoline had been cached along the way, and the passengers had to do road repair as they went along. The autos wore out nine tires, which were later exhibited by the U.S. Rubber Company to demonstrate their durability. Needless to say, there wasn't a rush of auto traffic to the North Rim after this expedition.

L TO R: *Woolley, Utah Senator Sutherland, and Utah Governor Thomas on North Rim, 1905*

He was fortunate to cross paths with many of the interesting historical characters who traveled through the region in the early twentieth century, such as Zane Grey and President Theodore Roosevelt.

True or not, his stories were always entertaining and made him a popular storyteller. Fortunately, many of his stories have been preserved in the book *The Roll Away Saloon: Cowboy Tales of the Arizona Strip*, written by Rider's granddaughter, Deirdra Paulsen.

NORTH KAIBAB RANGER DISTRICT

Most of the Kaibab Plateau's land was set aside as the Grand Canyon Forest Reserve by President Benjamin Harrison in 1893, and renamed Kaibab National Forest in 1908. This act did not preclude grazing, mining, and lumbering. President Theodore Roosevelt created the Grand Canyon Game Preserve in 1906, which includes more than 612,000 acres (247,676 hectares) of the Kaibab National Forest, noting that they were to be "set aside for the protection of game animals and birds." In 1965, 200,000 acres (80,940 hectares) of the Kaibab National Forest were designated as Kaibab Squirrel Area, a National Natural Landmark created specifically to protect the habitat of this endemic squirrel. Today this land is managed by the North Kaibab Ranger District of the USDA Forest Service.

LEFEVRE OVERLOOK

Within the North Kaibab Ranger District of the Kaibab National Forest, is the Lefevre Overlook, named after an early local ranching family. This is a good place to stop and take in

The Grand
Staircase

the panoramic view to the north toward Utah. On a clear day, you can see from the Glen Canyon National Recreation Area in the east to Zion National Park in the west, and north to the Beaver Mountains.

To the north, a series of ascending cliffs rise like a staircase, a grand staircase, much of which is included in the Grand Staircase–Escalante National Monument. Each step represents millions of years of geologic time. Underfoot is the limestone of the Kaibab Formation, the same layer that makes up the rim of the Grand Canyon. The limestone slopes gently downward to the north and underlies all that you see.

Looking beyond the slope of pinyon–juniper woodland below, the risers of the staircase are known locally as the Chocolate Cliffs (Moenkopi Formation), Vermilion Cliffs (Moenave Formation), White Cliffs (Navajo Sandstone), Gray Cliffs (various Cretaceous formations), and Pink Cliffs (Claron Formation). The Moenkopi Formation is about 230 million years old and the top Claron Formation is roughly 45 million, a perfect example of the "layer cake" makeup of the Colorado Plateau's geology—younger rocks atop older rocks.

There may be Navajo craftspeople selling their wares at this overlook. These venders work under a permit system authorized by the North Kaibab Ranger District.

From Leferve Overlook, the highway continues southward, gaining elevation until ponderosa pines begin to dominate the forest landscape.

SCENIC

U.S. Highway 89A

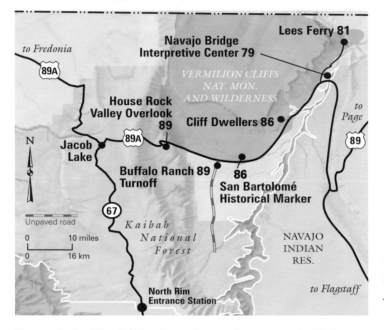

Numbers on the map refer to page numbers for information about the area.

To reach the North Rim from the south or east take U.S. Highway 89 through the western section of the vast Navajo Indian Reservation to the U.S. Highway 89A turnoff. If you happen to be coming from the Glen Canyon National Recreation Area and Page, this turnoff will be at the base of the switchbacks that bring you to the Marble Platform.

As the modern Highway 89A parallels the cliffs, it follows closely the old Mormon Emigrant Wagon Road from Utah (aka The Arizona Road or Honeymoon Trail), which traces even earlier Native American paths. There is little hint of a great canyon to the west until U.S. Highway 89A bridges the Colorado River at Marble Canyon, the name John Wesley Powell gave to the upper reaches of the Grand Canyon.

The highway then swings around the base of the towering Vermilion Cliffs, shooting across the Marble Platform before beginning the steep climb up the wavelike crustal fold called the East Kaibab monocline. From desert grassland dotted with rabbitbrush, big sage, broom snakeweed, and salt bush, the road ascends through pinyon pine and juniper woodland, which is replaced with ponderosa pine forest as the road climbs in elevation. Once on top of the Kaibab Plateau, turn south onto Arizona Highway 67 at Jacob Lake for the 45-mile (72.4-km) journey past the recovering remains of the 2006 Warm Fire, then through the lovely mixed conifer and aspen forest broken by verdant meadows.

NAVAJO BRIDGE INTERPRETIVE CENTER

Prior to 1929, the recommended route for driving an automobile from the South Rim of the Grand Canyon to the North Rim was to first go south to the unpaved Route 66, then west to Kingman, Arizona, then northwest and cross the Colorado River at Searchlight, Nevada, then continue north and northeast to St. George, Utah, then east to Kanab and finally south to Bright Angel Point, a trip of more than 600 dusty, bone-jarring miles (966 km) to end up only 10 air miles (16 km) from where you started.

In January 1929, a bridge spanning Marble Canyon was completed; and although the road was unpaved until 1938, more and more intrepid motorists began to follow the shorter route around the eastern side of the Grand Canyon, following

in the wagon-wheel ruts of the Mormon pioneers. This journey was "only" a third of the 600-mile (966-km) one.

Marble Canyon contains no marble, but rather polished limestone. When John Wesley Powell floated down the Colorado River in 1869, he wrote,

"And now the scenery is on a grand scale. The walls of the canyon, 2,500 feet [762 m] high, are of marble, of many beautiful colors, often polished below by the waves, and sometimes far up the sides, where showers have washed the sands over the cliffs. At one place I have a walk for more than a mile on a marble platform, all polished and fretted with strange devices and embossed in a thousand fantastic patterns. Through a cleft in the wall the sun shines on this pavement and it gleams in iridescent beauty . . . we call it Marble Canyon."

When you cross Marble Canyon on the U.S. Highway 89A bridge, notice that there is a second bridge to the north (upstream). This is the original 1929 Navajo Bridge. On the east side is the Navajo Indian Reservation and a pullout where you may find locals selling arts and crafts. On the west side is a parking area for the Navajo Bridge Interpretive Center operated by the Glen Canyon Natural History Association. This is a great place to acquire information, maps, books, and other material about the area. Between the southwest end of the historic bridge and the interpretive center is a rock structure built by the Civilian Conservation Corps during the Great Depression as a "road stop."

The Navajo Bridge provides the only opportunity for vehicles to cross the Colorado River along its 277-mile course through the Grand Canyon.

Take a few minutes to walk out onto the old bridge for a view of the Colorado River far below. You may spy boaters floating down the river. This is also a good place to think about what has happened to the Colorado River over the last fifty years or so. About 20 river miles (32 km) upstream is the Glen Canyon Dam. Since its completion in 1963, the Colorado River below the dam has changed dramatically. Instead of a red desert torrent "too thick to drink yet too thin to plow," it is now a clear (except during heavy storm runoff), cold river whose depth fluctuates according to the whims and wishes of power and irrigation companies. Before the dam, the wild Colorado River was always muddy . . . and sometimes raging. What you see today is a tamed, regulated river.

The eight native fish species, six of which are endemic to the Colorado River system, have suffered from the changed riverine conditions. Four species are now gone from the Grand Canyon section of the river, and the remaining four are endangered. In their place is an exotic species—the rainbow trout. The natives laid eggs that required warm water for hatching. Now those waters, released from the depths of Lake Powell, run cold. Non-native trout have been planted, and

these voracious predators feed upon any hatchlings that might come along.

Although trout stocking began in a few of the clear, cool side creeks in the Grand Canyon as early as 1919, these planted fish could not move out into the muddy, warm Colorado. However, after Glen Canyon Dam was completed, trout could be released directly into the main-stem river. The trout have done phe-nomenally well in the clear, cold water, and anglers test their skills between Lees Ferry and Glen Canyon Dam, all part of Glen Canyon National Recreation Area, which includes Lake Powell, as well.

LEES FERRY

The original Navajo Bridge (right) is open for foot traffic.

Turn onto the spur road to Lees Ferry, just beyond the west end of Navajo Bridge. A 6-mile (9.7-km), scenic drive takes you to the ferry site, sometimes referred to as the crossroads of northern Arizona. Over the years, Lees Ferry became, as writer Frank Waters called it, "Geographically our 42nd and Broadway. . . . For nearly four centuries everybody has even-tually showed up here." This is where the Colorado River emerges from one canyon, Glen, before plunging into the next, Marble. At Lees Ferry there is about a 2-mile (3.2-km) stretch where it is relatively easy to reach the bank of the Colorado River. This ease of access won't occur again until 225 miles (362 km) downstream.

Lees Ferry is the launch site for river trips through the Grand Canyon.

In mid-winter, 1776, Spanish padres Silvestre Vélez de Escalante and Francisco Atanasio Domínguez attempted to cross the Colorado River here, close to where the Paria River enters the main channel. "To do this, two of those who knew

how to swim well entered the river naked with their clothes upon their heads. It was so deep and wide that the swimmers, in spite of their prowess, were barely able to reach the other side, leaving in midstream their clothing, which they never saw again. And since they became so exhausted getting there, nude and barefoot, they were unable to walk far enough to do said exploring, coming back across after having paused a while to catch their breath."

They seemed to be trapped. "We are surrounded on all sides by mesas and big hogbacks impossible to climb." Understandably discouraged, they named their camp San Benito de Salsipuedes, "Get out if you can." However, they eventually located a route just a short distance up the Paria River that led over the cliffs and back down to an easier crossing further up the Colorado. (This adventuresome route is occasionally used today by hikers. Check with the Lees Ferry ranger for directions and precautions.)

Other travelers passed this way. In 1908's *The Last of the Plainsmen*, western author Zane Grey wrote,

> *"I saw the constricted rapids, where the Colorado took its plunge into the box-like head of the Grand Cañon . . . and the deep, reverberating boom of the river, at flood height, was a fearful thing to hear. I could not repress a shudder at the thought of crossing above that rapid."*

John D. Lee's ferry in mid-river, 1925

Even crossing the unruly Colorado by ferry was exciting and sometimes dangerous. As the Navajo Bridge was being constructed in 1928, two passengers and the ferryman Adolph Johnson were drowned when the ferry torqued and flipped in a whirlpool.

Arizona historian Sharlot Hall observed in 1911, "We dropped down over a lot of hills that seemed made out of all the scrapings of the Painted Desert and saw a big copper line like a badly twisted snake crawling along below with the greenest fields I ever saw beyond it and the reddish cliffs behind them. . . . It was as beautiful as it was wild and strange and I doubt if there is a wilder, stranger spot in the Southwest."

In August 1940, a young, not-yet-senator Barry Goldwater arrived at Lees Ferry on a river trip guided by Norman Nevills. Goldwater remarked, "Beautiful, historic, restful—Lees Ferry always has been one of my favorite spots."

John Doyle Lee with two of his wives, circa 1875

So, who was this Lee character? In 1857, a wagon train passing through Mountain Meadows, southwest of Cedar City, Utah, was attacked by the Utah Militia (and possibly Paiute Indians) who killed about 120 men, women, and children. Only seventeen young children were spared. The reasons and events that led up to this massacre are complex, but suffice it to say that the Mormon participants in this event thought they were protecting their families. Others saw it as a brutal, unjustifiable act. Only one person was ever singled out and punished for the crime—John Doyle Lee.

The Mormon Church suggested that Lee make himself scarce, so he headed off into the wilds of southern Utah. He established the

PEARL GRAY

In 1906 Pearl Gray, a struggling author whose daytime job was dentistry, attended a lecture given by Charles Jesse "Buffalo" Jones telling about his cattalo experiments and roping mountain lions at the Grand Canyon. (Read more about Jones on page 89.) While most of the audience was incredulous, Pearl was riveted by these tales. Introductions were forthcoming and plans made.

The next spring, Pearl stepped off the train in Flagstaff, where Jones was waiting for him. They rode north on horseback along the base of the Echo Cliffs, crossed the Colorado River at Lees Ferry, and continued to Jones's ranch, where Pearl photographed one of the cattalos (the offspring of a bison and domestic cow). Finally, it was time to ride up onto the Kaibab Plateau and to a detached sky-island within the Grand Canyon known as the Powell Plateau. Jones proclaimed that the isolated Powell Plateau was the breeding ground for hundreds of lions that ". . . infest the North Rim of the canyon," and that no white man or Indian had ever hunted lions there.

The party used dogs to track, chase, and eventually tree a lion. Then Jones and the others roped the terrified critter while trying to stay clear of the cat's sharp claws and teeth. The lion's feet were tied, claws clipped, and mouth muzzled. Six lions were captured alive, several were killed, and many escaped.

Gray returned home and fired off several articles, stories, and a book, *The Last of the Plainsmen*, based on his Grand Canyon adventures. The reading public began to take notice of this new author, who changed the spelling of his surname from Gray to Grey and dropped his effeminate first name in favor of his manlier middle one: Zane.

Homestead cabin at Lonely Dell

ferry and ranch at the head of the Grand Canyon near the mouth of the Paria River. Back in 1858 Jacob Hamblin, a Mormon scout, explorer, and missionary, had reported that there was good land in this remote spot and named it "Lonely Dell."

When Lee and part of his large extended family arrived on December 12, 1871, polygamist Lee's seventeenth wife Emma agreed with Hamblin's appellation and the name stuck. Fugitive Lee actually spent little time there, constantly moving to keep out of the reach of the law; Emma became the main driving force behind the ferry and ranch. A month later, on January 29, the ferry had its first customers when a band of fifteen Navajos called from the east side for a ride. However, the only boat they had was an old flatboat, the *Cañon Maid*, abandoned by Powell. Lee's sixth wife Rachel volunteered to steer the flimsy craft while Lee rowed.

Not until the following year was a proper ferry boat constructed and launched. One important reason for maintaining a ferry at this location is that the Mormon Church leaders were concerned that their people might be forced to move from Utah to more tolerant Mexico, in part because of the practice of polygamy. A ferry here would aid in the exodus.

Work team at Lees Ferry, 1910

Ultimately, Lee was caught and after two trials (the first ended in a hung jury), Lee was sentenced to be shot by firing squad in Mountain Meadows. His grave is in Panguitch, Utah.

Besides visiting the historic Lonely Dell Ranch area and the ferry sites, there are two moderate hikes well worth considering. One descends Cathedral Wash about 1.5 miles (2.4 km) to a sandy beach on the river and is popular with fishermen.

The other is the Spencer Trail that ascends the cliffs about one-half mile (0.8 km) upstream from the Lees Ferry parking area. Follow the path that parallels the river. The Spencer Trail begins just about opposite the wreckage of the boat the *Charles H. Spencer*. The trail wastes no time in switchbacking 1.5 miles (2.4 km) up the Vermilion Cliffs, giving the hiker superlative views of the river and the head of Marble Canyon, the dramatic beginning of the Grand Canyon.

The trail is named after Charles H. Spencer, one of the more colorful prospectors and entrepreneurs of canyon country. Gold was known to occur in small quantities in the green shales of the Chinle Formation at the base of the Vermilion Cliffs. Spencer's plan was to set up a system of hydraulic hoses to shoot Colorado River water at the shale slopes and then send the dissolved material down a long flume to an amalgamator. He built this mule trail in 1910 to transport coal from Warm Creek, some 28 miles (45 km) north, to Lees Ferry. The coal was going to be used in powering pumps and sluices. But after the trail was completed, he decided that the mule trains could not carry enough coal, so another scheme was hatched.

Spencer hauled in a dismantled 92-foot-long paddle-wheel steamboat and reconstructed it at the mouth of Warm Creek. The boat was christened the *Charles H. Spencer*, loaded with coal, and sent to Lees Ferry. Unfortunately, Spencer discovered that much of the coal the boat could carry would be needed just to make the round trip. By this time, though, tests showed that the amount of gold in the Chinle shale was too small to be profitable. The *Charles H. Spencer* was moored and eventually sank. Undaunted, Spencer continued to prospect unsuccessfully in the area for more than fifty years seeking his El Dorado.

From Lees Ferry to the Kaibab Plateau, the highway closely follows the base of the towering Vermilion Cliffs. In 1984, these cliffs and Paria Canyon were designated a wilderness area; and then in 2000, the wilderness plus the remote Paria Plateau became the 294,000-acre (118,982-hectare)

Spencer's gold processing rig at Lees Ferry, 1911

The Echo Cliffs flank Highway 89 and parallel the Colorado River below Lees Ferry.

Vermilion Cliffs National Monument. More information and hiking permits for Paria Canyon and the Coyote Buttes area can be obtained online or at the Lees Ferry ranger station.

CLIFF DWELLERS

As the road skirts around the head of Soap Creek, you may notice what looks like a collection of ancient dwellings tucked next to and under oversized boulders. These are actually the remains of an early homestead and tourist attraction. In 1927, New Yorker Blanche Russell's car broke down near here. While awaiting rescue, she fell in love with the grandiose scenery and decided to buy a parcel. Several years later, she and her husband Bill constructed the little stone buildings to attract tourists.

SAN BARTOLOMÉ HISTORICAL MARKER

About 19 miles (30.5 km) west of the Navajo Bridge is the scenic San Bartolomé Historic Turnout.

In 1776, two Spanish padres, Fray Francisco Atanasio Domínguez and Fray Francisco Silvestre Vélez de Escalante, attempted to reach the missions in Monterey, California. But they left Santa Fe, New Mexico, too late in the year; by the time they reached the Great Basin region of western Utah, winter snows were beginning to close the high mountain passes. Instead of retracing their steps, their Indian guides took them on a route that ran south toward the Grand Canyon and then east to avoid the gorge. As they crossed the Arizona Strip, they encountered the Southern Paiute people who provided them with food and showed them the way across the strip. The Spaniards camped near this spot on the night of October 24, 1776. Naming it San Bartolomé, they wrote in their journal:

> *"Here there is extensive valley land but of bad terrain, for what is not sand is a kind of ground having about three inches of rubble, and after that loose soil of different hues there are many deposits of transparent gypsum, some of mica, and there also seem to be some of metallic ore."*

As you look toward the cliffs, a major indentation marks the approximate location of natural springs, variously known as Jacob's Pools or Rachel's Pools. Late in 1872, Lee was advised

that he would be safer at Jacob's Pools than down by the Colorado River. So he took Rachel, her family, and most of his cattle there and built another ranch, which he called Doyle's Retreat. But he didn't linger here long, preferring to maintain a low profile, be somewhat elusive, and visit his other wives.

By using binoculars you may glimpse very large birds catching updrafts along the upper edge of the cliffs; these are California condors. The largest flying land bird in North America is once again soaring over the Grand Canyon region after a close brush with extinction. California condors weigh up to 26 pounds (11.8 kg) and have a wingspan up to 9.5 feet (3 m). Juveniles, which are as big as adults by the time they fledge, have dark-colored heads and

Vermilion Cliffs

black bills until they are three to four years old. Then they acquire a pinkish-orange, featherless head and ivory-colored bill. They may live to be sixty years old but the females lay only a single egg every other year or so. Condors were once thought to be closely related to raptors (hawks) but DNA analysis has shown that storks are their closest relatives.

In prehistoric times, condors ranged from Canada to Mexico, and fossil evidence shows that condors have been nesting in the Grand Canyon region for at least 50,000 years. A dramatic decrease in their numbers occurred at the end of

California condors have been successfully reintroduced from a release site above the Vermilion Cliffs.

the last ice age, when many of their food items, such as dead and decaying mastodons, giant ground sloths, and camels, went extinct. After the mid-1880s, Arizona had only scattered reports of condors. The last known active nest was observed near Lees Ferry in the 1890s. The last sighting of a condor in Arizona was one near Williams in 1924. By 1982, only twenty-two wild condors remained in all of North America.

Through a successful captive-breeding program, the condor population reached nearly 300 birds in 2006. Reintroductions began in 1992 in California, 1996 in Arizona, and 2003 in Baja California, Mexico. Each released bird has been fitted with a radio transmitter and numbered wing tag, and biologists monitor them daily.

RAPTOR MIGRATION

IN 1987, field biologist Chuck LaRue noted that the fall migration of hawks and other raptors along the intermountain migratory flyway from Alaska to Mexico streams right over the Grand Canyon region. Since the early 1990s, observers for HawkWatch International have been conducting surveys of migrating raptors over the Grand Canyon. Being at the top of the food pyramid, healthy raptor populations indicate healthy prey populations and presumably healthy habitats. Migration counts are an efficient and economical method for monitoring the regional status of raptors, which serve as important indicators of ecosystem health.

During migration, raptors rely on thermal uplifts and ridgeline updrafts to help them conserve energy. The migration over the Grand Canyon is rather unique in that the migrants are not guided by mountain ridges but strictly by the utilization of thermals. Southbound migrants travel over the Kaibab Plateau, which provides plenty of cover for roosting and hunting. The Painted Desert to the east is avoided perhaps because of its inhospitable conditions. Many of the migrants seem to be guided out along the narrow peninsulas of North Rim protruding into the canyon and then head for northward-pointing fingers along the South Rim, such as Lipan and Yaki points.

Sharp-shinned hawks, Cooper's hawks, red-tailed hawks, and American kestrels are the four species most commonly recorded. One observation that concerns the biologists is an apparent decrease in golden eagles.

After a hiatus of more than a century, condors are once again nesting in the Grand Canyon. During the spring of 2001, a condor laid an egg in a secluded cave near the North Rim. Unfortunately, the inexperienced parents broke the egg. Two years later, a chick managed to hatch and fledge; but this young bird died in 2005, probably of malnutrition. Two more fledged in 2004 and an increase in the number of active nests is a hopeful sign that the birds are adjusting well and increasing in numbers. It has been a long, difficult struggle, but the survival of this unique creature in the wild now seems assured.

BUFFALO RANCH TURNOFF

Several miles west of the San Bartolomé Historic Turnout, an unpaved road leads 22 miles (35.4 km) south to the Buffalo Ranch. Here in House Rock Valley roam a herd of American bison (popularly called buffalo). The buffalo are here through the efforts of Charles Jesse "Buffalo" Jones, an ex-buffalo hunter. By the end of the nineteenth century, the wild buffalo was nearing extinction, and Jones became concerned. In earlier days, he had taken advantage of the booming market for buffalo hides and meat, but became angered by the merciless waste and put away his rifle. Instead, Jones turned to roping buffalo calves and breeding them in hopes of perpetuating the species.

He also had a dream of crossing bison bulls with black Scottish Galloway cows to produce a hybrid animal possessing the virtues of each parent, namely silky hair; rich, tender meat; immunity to disease; the ability to survive harsh weather; and the capacity to eat meager, scrubby browse. Through his friendship with President Theodore Roosevelt, Jones received a federal permit in January 1906 to fence a large area on the Kaibab Plateau for buffalo (even though buffalo are not native to this area) and other big game animals. Later that same year, Roosevelt established the Grand Canyon National Game Preserve, which included the entire Kaibab Plateau.

Furthermore, the Secretary of Agriculture wrote a letter to the Secretary of the Interior, allowing Jones to obtain a loan of buffalo from Yellowstone ". . . for the purpose of experimenting in the hybridizing of buffalo and cattle, the Government to retain a certain percentage of the produce."

By issuing stock certificates, Jones was able to raise money to purchase Scottish Galloway cows and additional buffalo. However, getting the animals to the Kaibab Plateau was no small feat. They arrived via train in Lund, Utah, the closest railhead at the time. But they had to cross more than 150 miles (241 km) of inhospitable desert to reach the cool forests of the Kaibab Plateau. The cows refused to walk during the heat of the day, so the wranglers coaxed them along at night with a wagon full of wheat.

Buffalo didn't thrive on the high plateau; soon the animals were moved to the lower grasslands of House Rock Valley. Producing the hybrids, or "cattalos" as Jones called them, proved to be challenging. The buffalo and Galloways bred reluctantly. Male calves from the first crossbreeding were either aborted or caused the death of the cow. The heifer calves survived but, when bred to buffalo bulls, produced sterile male calves because the thick coats of the latter kept the reproductive organs at too high a temperature. Only by breeding back to domestic cattle could fertile males be obtained.

Jim Owens tending his herd

Unfortunately for Jones, all the experimenting took too long and his investors attempted to recoup their losses by claiming the domestic animals. One old cattalo, with a definite buffalo body shape but covered with blotches of white fur, was put on display at Jacob Lake and tourists paid 50¢ to see it.

Jim Owens, the forest service game warden, eventually took over the herd, but in the 1920s sold them to the state of Arizona. Today, the Arizona Game and Fish Department maintains the herd at about 100 animals and recent genetic testing confirms that they still carry the domestic cattle genes. Hunts are held once a year on a lottery basis. It's considered one of the toughest hunts in the state because of the difficulty in locating the animals. Hunters are more likely to see pronghorn and jackrabbits.

Though the buffalo (or cattalo) are supposed to be contained within their game range, which covers about 60,000 acres (24,282 hectares) of sagebrush and grassland, they occasionally wander into the adjacent Kaibab National Forest and Grand Canyon National Park, much to the rangers' chagrin. The animals are not native to the area and do considerable damage to vegetation as well as polluting water sources. And while they may appear to be slow-moving animals, they can easily outrun a person. Never approach them on foot.

HOUSE ROCK VALLEY OVERLOOK

Getting to the top of the Kaibab Plateau in a motorized vehicle used to be a much more difficult undertaking than it is today. Before the 1930s, the road climbing the East Kaibab monocline was much steeper. Autos of the early twentieth century had gravity-fed gas lines; ascending a steep hill meant that gas wouldn't flow to the engine. The problem was "solved" by driving backwards.

House Rock Valley was named after a campsite near a spring at the base of the Vermilion Cliffs, where a couple of large boulders lean together to form a crude shelter. Sometime prior to 1871, someone using a piece of charcoal printed the name Rock House Hotel on one of the rocks. Several members of the second Powell expedition noted the inscription and added the name to their map.

While gazing across the broad Marble Platform, coyotes, pronghorn antelope, and bison may come to mind, but a host of smaller creatures also call the desert grasslands home. One of these is the northern grasshopper mouse, which has been described as "howling like a wolf and attacking like a lion." That might be a bit of an exaggeration for the diminutive grasshopper mouse, which measures only five or

six inches from nose to tip of tail. However, its behavior *is* quite different from most other mice.

Grasshopper mice rear up on their hind legs, use their tail for balance, point their head upwards, and emit a tiny squeak, the so-called howl. Then they're off searching for food—not seeds and vegetation like other mice—but invertebrates, reptiles, and even the occasional rodent up to three times their size. Cannibalism is not uncommon either. The actions of these aggressive and combative mice have been likened to those of shrews. Thus the phrase, "Be a man or be a mouse" takes on new significance.

Continue along Highway 89A as it climbs the East Kaibab monocline, rising to 8,000 feet (2,400 m) in elevation as you reach Jacob Lake.

APPENDIX A:
SUGGESTED READING

Abbott, Lon, and Terri Cook. *Hiking the Grand Canyon's Geology*. Seattle: The Mountaineers Books, 2004.

Aitchison, Stewart. *Grand Canyon: Window of Time*. Mariposa: Sierra Press, 1999.

Anderson, Michael F. *Living at the Edge: Explorers, Exploiters and Settlers of the Grand Canyon Region*. Grand Canyon: Grand Canyon Association, 1998.

Anderson, Michael F. *Polishing the Jewel: An Administrative History of Grand Canyon National Park*. Grand Canyon: Grand Canyon Association, 2000.

Bagley, Will. *Blood of the Prophets: Brigham Young and the Massacre at Mountain Meadows*. Norman: University of Oklahoma Press, 2004

Bailey, Florence Merriam. *Among the Birds in the Grand Canyon Country*. Washington, D.C.: U.S. Government Printing Office, 1939.

Billingsley, George H., Earle E. Spamer, and Dove Menkes. *Quest for the Pillar of Gold: The Mines & Miners of the Grand Canyon*. Grand Canyon: Grand Canyon Association, 1997.

Brown, Bryan T., Steven W. Carothers, and R. Roy Johnson. *Grand Canyon Birds*. Tucson: University of Arizona Press, 1987.

Coder, Christopher M. An *Introduction to Grand Canyon Prehistory*. Grand Canyon: Grand Canyon Association, 2000.

Crampton, C. Gregory, ed. *Sharlot Hall on the Arizona Strip*. Prescott: Sharlot Hall Museum Press, 1999.

Easton, Robert and Mackenzie Brown. *Lord of the Beasts: The Saga of Buffalo Jones*. Tucson: University of Arizona Press, 1961.

Grey, Zane. *The Last of the Plainsmen*. New York: Grosset & Dunlap, 1908.

Holt, Ronald L. *Beneath These Red Cliffs: An Ethnology of the Utah Paiutes*. Albuquerque: University of New Mexico Press, 1992.

Houk, Rose. *An Introduction to Grand Canyon Ecology*. Grand Canyon: Grand Canyon Association, 1996.

Lago, Don. "The Toquerville Myth." *Boatman's Quarterly Review*. 16:3.

Leach, Nicky. *Pipe Spring National Monument*. Springdale: Zion Natural History Association, 1999.

Leavengood, Betty. *Grand Canyon Women: Lives Shaped by Landscape*. Grand Canyon: Grand Canyon Association, 2004.

Martineau, LaVan. *Southern Paiute Legends: Legends, Lore, Language, and Lineage*. Las Vegas: KC Publications, 1992.

Pauly, Thomas H. *Zane Grey: His Life, His Adventures, His Women*. Champaign: University of Illinois Press, 2005.

Powell, James Lawrence. *Grand Canyon: Solving Earth's Grandest Puzzle*. Upper Saddle River, N.J.: Pearson Education, Inc., 2005.

Price, Edna. *Burro Bill and Me*. Death Valley: Death Valley Natural History Association, 1993.

Price, L. Greer. *An Introduction to Grand Canyon Geology*. Grand Canyon: Grand Canyon Association, 1999.

Ranney, Wayne. *Carving Grand Canyon: Evidence, Theories, and Mystery*. Grand Canyon: Grand Canyon Association, 2005.

Reilly, P.T. *Lees Ferry from Mormon Crossing to National Park*. Logan: Utah State University Press, 1999.

Rider, Rowland W., with Dierdre Paulsen. *The Roll Away Saloon: Cowboy Tales of the Arizona Strip*. Logan: Utah State University Press, 1985.

Schmidt, Jeremy. *A Natural History Guide: Grand Canyon National Park*. New York: Houghton Mifflin Company, 1993.

Schwartz, Douglas W. *On the Edge of Splendor: Exploring Grand Canyon's Human Past*. Santa Fe: School of American Research, n.d.

Stegner, Wallace. *Beyond the Hundredth Meridian: John Wesley Powell and the Second Opening of the West*. New York: Penguin Books, 1954.

Warner, Ted J., ed. *The Domínguez-Escalante Journal: Their Expedition through Colorado, Utah, Arizona, and New Mexico in 1776*. Salt Lake City: University of Utah Press, 1995.

APPENDIX B:
INFORMATION RESOURCES

Navajo Bridge Interpretive Center
West of Navajo Bridge on
U.S. Highway 89A; 928-355-2319
www.nps.gov/glca/historyculture/
navajobridge.htm

Kaibab Plateau Visitor Center
Jacob Lake, Fredonia, AZ 86022;
928-643-7298; www.fs.fed.us/r3/kai/visit/
visit.html

North Kaibab Ranger District
P.O. Box 248, Fredonia, AZ 86022;
928-643-7395; www.fs.fed.us/r3/kai/visit/
visit.html

Pipe Spring National Monument
HC 65, Box 5, Fredonia, AZ 86022;
928-643-7105; www.nps.gov/pisp

North Rim Visitor Center: Pick up a copy
of the free *The Guide* and *Trip Planner* for
more detailed information on camping,
lodging, restaurants, ranger programs, etc.

Grand Canyon National Park
P.O. Box 129, Grand Canyon, AZ 86023;
www.nps.gov/grca

Navajo Nation Parks and Recreation
Department
P.O. Box 9000,
Window Rock, AZ 86515;
www.navajoland.com

BLM Arizona Interagency
Information Office
345 East Riverside Drive,
St. George, UT 84790-9000;
(435) 688-3200; www.blm.gov/az/

Arizona Game and Fish Department,
Region II Office
3500 S. Lake Mary Road,
Flagstaff, AZ 86001, 928-774-5045;
www.azgfd.com

ABOUT THE AUTHOR

Stewart Aitchison has been exploring,
studying, and writing about the
Grand Canyon region for more than
four decades. Some of his other books
include *Grand Canyon: Window of Time,
A Naturalist's Guide to Hiking the Grand
Canyon, A Wilderness Called Grand
Canyon, A Traveler's Guide to Monument
Valley,* and *A Guide to Southern Utah's
Hole-in-the-Rock Trail.* He lives in
Flagstaff, Arizona.

ACKNOWLEDGMENTS

Putting together a guide consisting of such a wide range of topics requires assistance from many different experts. I was very fortunate in receiving this help and hope that I have interpreted their contributions correctly and clearly.

I would like to thank Bruce Aiken, Jennie Albrinck, Mike Anderson, Michelle Bailey, Jan Balsom, Emma Benenati, Don Bertolette, Andrea Bornemeier, Paula Branstner, Ellen Brennan, Angelita Bulletts, Julie Crawford, Dennis Curtis, Diane Doyle, Charles Drost, Christopher Eaton, Helen Fairley, Pam Frazier and the staff of Grand Canyon Association, Pete Fulé, Amy Horn, Martha Kreuger, Don Lago, Mark & Mary McCutcheon, Margaret Moore, Rick Moore, Carol Ogburn, Deidre Paulsen, Tom Pittenger, Richard Quartaroli, Wayne Ranney, Donn Reynard, Mandy Reynard, Doug Schwartz, Ellen Seeley, Judy Springer, Amanda Summers, Robin Tellis, Bill Torres, Scott Thybony, John Vankat, Kate Watters, Marion Werthington, Jim Wessel, Pam Whipple, Stuart Whipple, Catherine Wightman, and Alana Woo.

Any statements of opinion or errors of fact are strictly my own.

PHOTOGRAPHY CREDITS

Bruce Aiken 28 bottom; Stewart Aitchison 37, 55 both, 59 bottom, 66, 71 bottom; Tom Bean 10 bottom, 11, 57, 70 bottom; Ron Blakey 44 both; Ron Bohr 45, 86 top; BYU, Harold B. Lee Library 75 both; Michael Collier 56 center, 58 bottom, 59 top, 69, 80, 87; Richard Demler 56 bottom right; Dick Dietrich 67 top; Michael Fogden Photography 91; Michael Francis 41 bottom; Grand Canyon National Park Museum Collection #17228, 12; #04453, 22; #05988, 23; 27; #05305 28 top; #06822, 29; #05427, 30; #09781, 31; clockwise from lower left #00577, #08144, #08148, #13469, #13637, 32; 33 bottom; 66204, 36; #10455, 42; #16001, 43; #05498, 48 top, #00175, 58; #17229, 63; #05877, 67 bottom; #31347 top, #05551 bottom 83; #02106, 90; Grand Canyon–Parashant National Monument 65, 68 bottom, 70 top, 71 top; Paul Gill 20, 35, 56 bottom left, 81 top; Bruce Griffin 8, 25 bottom; Kenneth Hamblin 38–39, 72–73; Dave Hammaker 33 top; Jeff Henry 60–61; Fred Hirschmann 15; George H. H. Huey 41 top, 56 top, 64; Liz Hymans 50–51, 76–77; Kaibab National Forest 54; Gary Ladd 52; Chuck Lawson 3, 49; Tom and Pat Leeson 24; Library of Congress, Geography and Map Division 13, 22; Bruce McHenry 26; Charles Melton 88; Natural Light Photography 81 bottom; NAU, Cline Library Special Collections and Archives 82, 84 bottom, 85; Laurence Parent 34; Douglas Schwartz 47; Sharlot Hall Museum, Prescott, Arizona 14, 15 bottom; Don Singer 25 top; Marc Solomon 68 top; David Welling cover, 4, 6, 17, 53; Leon Werdinger 79, 84 top; Kathryn Wilde 19, 86 bottom; U.S. Geological Survey 9, 10 top.

INDEX

Page numbers in *italics* indicate pictures or illustrations

95